OBEDIENTLY WE

This book is a work of critical non-fiction. It examines social, political, economic, religious, and ideological systems from historical, philosophical, and rational perspectives. All references to institutions, beliefs, or historical events are intended for analysis and critique, not defamation or incitement. The opinions expressed in this book are solely those of the author and do not represent any organization, institution, government, or authority.

This book does not promote hatred, violence, or discrimination against any individual or group. Its purpose is to encourage critical thinking, ethical reflection, and intellectual autonomy.

ISBN: 978-93-5679-056-8
Obediently We, Eleven Fifty Publishing

Contact Information:
xettyee@gmail.com
elevenfiftypublishing@gmail.com

Disclaimer

This book is a work of critical non-fiction intended for intellectual, philosophical, and educational purposes. It examines human behavior, social systems, institutions, ideologies, and historical events through rational, analytical, and evidence-based perspectives. The discussions presented herein focus on structures of power, obedience, authority, and belief systems, rather than on individuals or personal identities.

All references to religion, nationalism, capitalism, governments, laws, institutions, cultures, or historical events are made strictly in a critical and academic context. The intent is to analyze how systems function, how obedience is produced and maintained, and how moral responsibility is often transferred from individuals to authority. These references should not be interpreted as personal attacks, defamation, or targeted accusations against any individual, community, or group.

This book does not advocate violence, hatred, discrimination, or harm of any kind. It does not encourage unlawful activity, rebellion, or civil disorder. Instead, it promotes critical thinking, ethical awareness, intellectual autonomy, and peaceful inquiry into the foundations of social order and human conduct.

The views and interpretations expressed in this book are solely those of the author and do not represent the opinions, beliefs, or positions of any organization, institution, government, religious body, political party, or ideological group. Readers are encouraged to engage with the material thoughtfully, skeptically, and independently, and to consult multiple sources when forming their own conclusions.

Historical examples and case studies discussed in this book are used to illustrate broader systemic patterns and psychological mechanisms. While every effort has been made to ensure accuracy, the author does not claim absolute completeness or infallibility. Any errors or omissions are unintentional and subject to correction in future editions.

This book challenges widely accepted narratives and beliefs. Such challenges may cause discomfort or disagreement. That discomfort is not the objective but a possible outcome of confronting deeply ingrained assumptions. Readers are free to disagree with the arguments presented and are encouraged to do so through reasoned dialogue rather than emotional reaction.

Nothing in this book should be interpreted as professional legal, medical, psychological, or financial advice. The content is not a substitute for professional consultation in any specialized field.

By reading this book, the reader acknowledges that ideas, critiques, and arguments presented are part of an ongoing intellectual exploration of human society and should be understood within that context. The ultimate responsibility for interpretation rests with the reader.

“We inherit rules before we inherit reason.”
— Alok Barman

TABLE OF CONTENTS

INTRODUCTION

The social world we live in is rarely seen as a 'constructed reality'. Law, education, work, family, state, and economy present themselves as natural, inevitable, and unquestionable. Rather than appearing as products of historical processes or power relations, these structures come to be seen as part of "normal life." Over time, they become so familiar that their presence fades from view—and this invisibility becomes their greatest strength.

This conditioning begins in childhood. Individuals are taught how to think, how to behave, how to follow discipline, how to respect authority, and how to define success. In the name of education, discipline, and progress, a framework is internalized in which adjustment is understood as maturity and obedience as responsibility. Yet a basic question is rarely asked: "in whose interest do these structures ultimately operate, and at whose cost?"

'Obediently We' is neither a manifesto nor a guide to reform. It does not prescribe an ideology, nor does it claim to offer solutions. It is an observation. This book examines the invisible structures that organize modern society while remaining largely unquestioned. Obedience is not treated here as an individual failure or moral weakness, but as a "systemic condition"—produced through social, economic, political, and cultural arrangements.

Most people do not obey because they lack the capacity to resist, but because obedience is tied to survival. Employment, income, housing, education, legality, and social legitimacy are all linked to compliance. To go against the system is not merely to disagree; it often entails the risk of instability, exclusion, and insecurity. In this context, obedience appears less as a conscious choice and more as an imposed condition.

At the center of this book lies a simple yet unsettling question:

"Do human beings truly live with free will, or do they exist within frameworks in which most of their choices have already been structured?"

Modern societies celebrate freedom, choice, and individuality as core values. Individuals are told that they are the architects of their own lives. Yet closer examination reveals that choices exist only within a limited, pre-approved range. The system defines the options; the individual merely selects among them. In this way, choice becomes a tool—creating the illusion of freedom while rendering the structure itself invisible.

Through this process, responsibility is shifted onto the individual. Failure appears personal rather than structural. Success is seen as the result of merit rather than conditioning. The system conceals its own limitations and assigns individuals responsibility for their position within it. The narrative of freedom masks power.

'Obediently We' attempts to show how power operates without constant coercion. Modern systems of control rely less on direct violence and more on fear of economic insecurity, dependence, social approval, moral conditioning, and the promise of stability. Over time, individuals begin to self-regulate—adjusting their speech, ambitions, and expectations in accordance with the system. When obedience becomes habitual, authority becomes invisible.

The focus of this book is not on individuals or institutions, but on "structures"—the patterns that shape thought, behavior, and meaning, and then present themselves as “common sense.” This book questions the assumed inevitability of those structures.

Importantly, 'Obediently We' offers no solutions. Because offering solutions often creates a new system—a new ideology, a new form of obedience. The task of this book is not to prescribe, but to expose. It places a mirror before the reader and leaves interpretation in their hands.

Structured Obedience

The question of whether human beings genuinely live by free will or function within a framework of obedience shaped by social, economic, and political structures remains central to modern philosophical inquiry. At a superficial level, human life appears to be governed by freedom: individuals make choices, select life paths, and accept responsibility for the outcomes of their decisions. However, a deeper examination reveals that much of what is perceived as free choice is, in fact, structured obedience—behavior conditioned by forces that operate largely beyond individual control.

The world into which a person is born is not a neutral or open field of possibilities. From birth onward, individuals enter a reality already organized by legal systems, economic relations, educational institutions, cultural norms, religious traditions, linguistic frameworks, and political boundaries. None of these foundational structures are chosen; they are inherited. These systems do not merely exist around the individual but actively shape perception, desire, behavior, and the range of conceivable actions. As a result, decisions are never made in isolation; they occur within boundaries that are pre-established and socially reinforced.

Within such conditions, obedience becomes normalized and often invisible. Individuals believe they are exercising freedom, yet the options available to them have already been filtered, ranked, and limited by structural constraints. In the modern world, human existence is therefore not primarily defined by autonomous self-determination, but by continuous negotiation within social, economic, and political frameworks that subtly govern both opportunity and imagination. Free will, in this context, functions less as an absolute condition and more as a constrained experience shaped by inherited systems of power and organization.

An individual finds themselves in a world where the major parameters of life such as place of birth, language, class, economic status, education, and identity—are already determined even before any conscious choice is possible. In this context, the concept of free will becomes a philosophical puzzle: does an individual truly possess free will, or is it merely an illusion operating within structures of obedience? Traditionally, free will has been based on the idea that individuals can make decisions independently and rationally. However, when we examine real-world conditions, this notion appears deeply problematic.

In a capitalist economy, working becomes a compulsion for survival; within political systems, compliance with rules and laws is often driven by the fear of punishment; and social norms isolate or stigmatize deviation. Under such conditions, an individual's "choices" are mostly constrained choices—the available options are only those permitted by the system. In this sense, free will is not absolute freedom but a limited space for maneuvering, one that exists entirely within a framework of obedience. Neuroscience and cognitive psychology further challenge the traditional concept of free will. Multiple studies suggest that the human brain initiates decisions at the neural level before they are consciously realized. Consciousness often constructs a narrative after the fact—"I chose this." From this perspective, an individual's sense of agency is largely a post-facto rationalization.

Thoughts, desires, and impulses are not consciously chosen by individuals; they emerge from biological conditioning, past experiences, and environmental stimuli. From birth, human life is embedded within multiple structures. Family, society, religion, the state, language, the economy, and education—all these systems shape behavior, values, and thought. This form of obedience may be described as structured obedience. It is not overt slavery, but invisible discipline. The individual does not even recognize it as an order; instead, it comes to be perceived as "natural."

These are some of the systems of modern society that actively amplify possessive impulses within human beings—impulses that are ultimately harmful to humanity. They normalize control, ownership, competition, and conformity, often at the cost of empathy, autonomy, and collective well-being.

1. Economic pressure and obedience
2. Legal and political structures
3. Social pressure and the politics of honor and shame
4. The construction of morality
5. Religious obedience
6. Nationalism and identity politics
7. Training in discipline through education
8. The relationship between language and thought
9. Obedience within the family
10. Gender roles
11. Discipline in love and marriage
12. Preferences shaped and controlled by media and algorithms, among others in the following chapters, I will examine some of these central pillars of modern society in detail. These pillars are often presented as natural, necessary, or even beneficial.

Below, I present several examples of the outcomes of structured obedience. When we study history carefully, these outcomes become clearly visible.

Whenever boundaries are drawn across a land in the course of history, it is not only maps that change—lives change with them. Land suddenly becomes "foreign," countries are transformed overnight, and neighbors are declared enemies. In this entire process, neither kings, nor leaders, nor those in power ever ask ordinary people what they want. Yet it is they who are forced to bear the consequences. They are compelled to abandon their homes, their soil, their memories, and flee. In the power games played at the top, those who die are rarely kings or leaders—those who die are always ordinary people, just like you and me.

History offers thousands of such examples where the cost of wars, partitions, riots, or political decisions has been paid solely by the common people. Yet, strangely, history often teaches us to read these events merely as "incidents." We are made to memorize dates, recite the names of treaties, and study lists of rulers and victors. What is rarely explained is why, in every era, it is the common person who is crushed. Why do most people suffer punishment without any personal fault? And why do some people remain on top through every system, every crisis, and every change?

It is here that a bitter truth of history reveals itself. Human beings live with the belief that their lives are the result of their own decisions. But history repeatedly shows that the most decisive choices are made long before a person is born. No child chooses the country of their birth, the family they are born into, or the social and economic conditions into which they open their eyes. Yet these very initial circumstances determine how far they will be allowed to go.

Some are born into environments where even making mistakes is permitted—where failure is treated as learning. Others are born into conditions where punishment follows even when they do things right. This is why the rewards of hard work are not the same for everyone. Still, instead of acknowledging this inequality, society constructs a convenient narrative—that everything is achieved through effort alone.

This narrative is popular because it keeps the system stable. The poor are told they are weak, that they did not try hard enough. The rich are told they are capable, that their success is entirely the result of merit. The truth, however, is that both were born into their respective positions—one into a place where opportunities existed, and the other into a place where opportunities were absent.

If a person does not choose their starting point, why does society expect the same outcomes from everyone? If the foundation of life is laid in advance, who decides the standards of right and wrong? Perhaps the answer lies in what humans consider their independent thinking. In reality, that thinking is taught to them by social frameworks and structures of power.

Thus, history is not merely a story of the past; it is a mirror of the system in which the ordinary human being still lives today—a system where decisions are made at the top, the price is paid at the bottom, and obedience is taught to be accepted as destiny.

In 1961, an experiment conducted at Yale University in the United States shook the moral understanding of modern society. The experiment was designed by social psychologist Stanley Milgram.

Ordinary citizens were invited to participate. They were told that it was a scientific study related to "learning and memory." The participants were assigned the role of "teacher," while the person seated opposite them was called the "learner." The rule was simple: if the learner gave an incorrect answer to a question, the teacher was to administer an electric shock. With each wrong answer, the intensity of the shock was to be increased.

At first, the shocks were mild. Gradually, however, the voltage was raised. As the shocks grew stronger, the person seated opposite began to scream in pain, plead with folded hands, and beg for the experiment to be stopped. At a certain point, the person stopped screaming altogether—a silence that participants often interpreted as unconsciousness or death. Despite this, a person present in the experiment room—a "scientist" wearing a white coat—continued to speak calmly and repeatedly said only this: "The experiment requires it. Please continue."

That white coat was no ordinary garment. It was a symbol of authority, knowledge, and legitimacy. Most participants displayed discomfort, anxiety, and moral hesitation. Many were sweating, their hands trembling; some even protested. But when they were reassured that "the responsibility is not yours, it is the experiment's," they continued administering the shocks.

The results were shocking. Nearly two-thirds of the participants went as far as delivering shocks that could potentially be fatal. This happened even when the person in front of them was clearly showing signs of severe pain. Later, it was revealed that the "learner" was actually an actor, and no real electric shocks were being administered. All the pain had been staged.

The true conclusion of this experiment was not that people are cruel. Rather, it was that ordinary people, when acting under the orders of legitimate authority, detach themselves from moral responsibility. Milgram called this the "agentic state"—a psychological condition in which an individual no longer sees themselves as a moral decision-maker, but merely as an instrument executing orders.

This experiment revealed that obedience is not simply the result of external pressure; it is deeply conditioned from within. When an order comes from an "authorized" source, individuals temporarily suspend their moral judgment. Instead of taking responsibility upon themselves, they transfer it to authority, the system, or the procedure.

The Yale experiment demonstrates that human beings can be subdued not only through physical force, but also through mental structures. When the responsibility to think is handed over to someone else, obedience becomes the most civilized—and the most dangerous—form of violence.

Society decides what is right and what is wrong, what is acceptable to think and what is not. From childhood, people are taught to obey elders. Do not question. Breaking rules is wrong. Gradually, the mind becomes conditioned to obey orders as soon as they are given—regardless of whether the one giving them is speaking the truth or not.

In the 1930s, Germany was not an abnormal society. The people who lived there were ordinary human beings—they loved their children, laughed and spoke with their neighbors, and earned their livelihoods through hard work. They were not born as murderers or monsters. Yet that very society became a silent witness to one of the most organized and inhumane genocides in history. This contradiction is the most terrifying question of modern civilization.

After the First World War, Germany was passing through a deep economic, social, and psychological crisis. Humiliation, unemployment, and insecurity had hollowed out society from within. In such a climate, the Nazi regime presented Jews as the "national enemy"—an enemy supposedly corroding the nation from within. This claim was neither scientific nor rational; it was a political construction built on fear and falsehood. But a society in crisis does not seek reason—it seeks simple answers, and power provided exactly that.

Through state propaganda, fabricated racial science, and nationalist morality, the idea was gradually implanted that the injustice inflicted upon Jews was not injustice at all, but a national duty. Most citizens neither actively participated in killing nor openly resisted it. They became spectators. They did not ask questions—are these people truly enemies? Can an entire community be declared criminal? This silence became the most essential condition for the crime itself.

History would later name it a crime—a crime against humanity. But at the time, it was framed as duty, obedience, and moral responsibility. This is precisely the point at which morality reveals its most dangerous form—when it becomes an instrument for obeying orders rather than for thinking.

Religion and state-manufactured morality operate through the same mechanism. They often do not encourage independent evaluation of right and wrong; instead, they decide whose suffering will be recognized as moral and whose suffering will be rendered invisible. When morality stops asking questions, it ceases to be compassion and becomes the language of power. Nazi Germany is an extreme example of this, but this tendency is not confined to any one country or era.

This history does not teach us that "people are inherently evil." Rather, it teaches us that obedience, fear, and collective identity can combine to turn ordinary human beings into participants in an inhumane system.

In 1692, Salem (Massachusetts) was a small, rigidly religious community where every aspect of life was governed by Christian doctrine. Illness, famine, the death of children, or any unusual occurrence was explained not through natural causes but through "demonic influence." In such a society, fear was not merely an emotion; it was a social currency.

Certain adolescent girls were reportedly observed exhibiting strange behavior—seizures, screaming, bodies stiffening. When physicians found no physical cause, the conclusion was drawn that they were under the influence of "witchcraft." The girls were then asked who was responsible for their condition. They named several women—mostly those who lived on the margins of society: widows, the poor, the isolated, or those considered socially awkward.

These accusations were treated not as rumors, but as divine signs. The courts accepted "spectral evidence"—the claim that the accused woman's spirit or shadow had appeared in dreams or visions to cause harm. Such evidence could neither be seen nor challenged.

The accused women were arrested, kept in prison for months, often in chains. They were expected to confess to being witches. Those who confessed were sometimes spared; those who refused were declared guilty. In this way, truth was replaced by obedience as the standard of justice.

Punishment was public. Women were hanged before crowds. The process was presented not as justice, but as a religious ritual—through which society claimed to purify itself. The crowd was not silent; it prayed, listened to sermons, and believed it was fulfilling the will of God.

The events in Salem were not the product of a single town or an exceptional society. Between the 15th and 18th centuries, "witch hunts" spread across many parts of Europe—Germany, France, England, and Switzerland—as an organized social process. Historical studies estimate that more than fifty thousand people were punished for witchcraft during this period, approximately 70 to 80 percent of them women. This figure itself indicates that the violence was not accidental, but structurally targeted.

In these societies, the "witch" was not a mysterious being, but a social category—constructed by power, religion, and collective fear. Those most often targeted were women who lived outside accepted social norms. Widows, who existed without male protection; women living alone, whose independence unsettled society; women knowledgeable in herbs or traditional medicine, whose knowledge lay outside the Church-controlled religious framework; and women who spoke, questioned, or refused to accept established norms of obedience—all were deemed "suspicious."

This suspicion was not personal but collectively produced. Through religious sermons, rumors, and pseudo-scientific beliefs, society was taught that such women were threats to social order. As a result, the violence inflicted upon them was not seen as violence, but as a process of social purification. Courts legitimized unscientific evidence, such as spirits appearing in dreams or visions, treating them as divine signs.

Punishments were public and symbolic—burning alive, hanging, or death by stoning. The purpose of these penalties was not merely to eliminate the accused, but to send a message to the entire society that obedience itself was morality. Crowds watched these punishments—sometimes praying, sometimes in silence—believing they were not witnessing a crime, but the fulfillment of a moral duty.

A crucial fact is that most people involved in this process did not consider themselves evil. They believed they were obeying orders, following religion, and standing with what society defined as "right."

Notably, those who carried out these punishments did not see themselves as cruel. They acted according to law, religion, and morality—or at least as they had been taught. This is why the events of Salem are not merely a story of superstition; they demonstrate how, when power, religion, and fear legitimize one another, society can accept even murder as a moral obligation.

This tragedy does not prove that the people of that society were born cruel or inhuman. Rather, it shows how fear, religious belief, and social pressure together mold human conscience into a fixed framework. When an idea is presented across generations as moral truth, questioning it itself begins to appear immoral. In such conditions, even violence can take on the form of virtue.

The events of Salem make it clear that society often gives individuals the illusion that their thinking is independent, while in reality it is socially constructed. People think what their era, culture, and power structures declare to be "normal" and "right." This is why history contains many acts that were not called crimes at the time, but duties.

In the 1950s, apartheid in South Africa was not merely a social practice; it was a system formally established and enforced by law. Under this system, Black people had separate buses, separate residential areas, separate schools, and their presence was restricted in every sphere of life. They were required to sit at the back of buses, were barred from entering central urban areas, and their voices were rendered politically insignificant. All of this occurred without constant overt violence, unfolding instead as part of an ordinary, everyday routine.

The most horrifying aspect of this system was not only that it was unjust, but that it had been made normal. Most members of the white community did not see themselves as oppressors. From childhood, they had been taught that this was the natural order, the proper social balance, and the rule of civilization itself. Schools, churches, media, and the legal system together legitimized the idea that discrimination based on skin color was not only right, but necessary.

For generations, this system went largely unquestioned. This was not because people were incapable of thinking, but because questioning itself had been turned into a social offense. Anyone who challenged the system was labeled anti-national, disruptive, or dangerous. Obedience was given the form of morality, while dissent was equated with chaos.

Apartheid demonstrates that oppression does not always arrive in a violent form. Often, it appears as law, etiquette, and "normal behavior." When injustice becomes a daily habit, it stops being visible. People participate in it, repeat it, and still consider themselves innocent—because they are simply doing what society expects of them.

In this sense, South African apartheid is not merely a story of racial discrimination. It is a story of obedience—of the mental conditioning through which people come to believe that whatever system exists must be right. When independent thought is mortgaged in exchange for social acceptance, injustice can survive for generations without resistance. History shows that human beings are conquered not by the sword, but by ideas. Once the mind bends, the body follows—and this is the most dangerous condition of all, because a person may not even realize when they began living according to someone else's thinking.

This leads to a deeper question: if our thinking itself is not fully in our own hands—if even our sense of right and wrong is taught to us—then who truly holds power in society? Who decides who remains above and who is pushed below? Perhaps the answer lies in that force before which thought, morality, and obedience all bow.

In 1943, Bengal was in the grip of famine. People were dying of hunger on the streets, children were breathing their last in their mothers' arms, and the elderly collapsed while walking, unable to rise again. This scene was not the result of a natural disaster. There was no shortage of grain—warehouses were full, ships stood docked at ports, and grain existed in the markets. Yet for ordinary people, that grain was out of reach.

This famine was not caused by a lack of rainfall, but by the priorities of the system itself. Wartime policies, hoarding, exports, and failures in price control turned grain into a commodity priced far beyond the purchasing power of the masses. Both the state and the market accepted that prices would be determined "naturally"—even if the consequence was mass death. Here, history exposed a disturbing truth: when hunger and money stand face to face, money often wins.

The most terrifying aspect of this tragedy was not simply that people were starving, but that it was considered legally, administratively, and morally normal. No one openly declared, "Let people die," yet policies were maintained that produced precisely that outcome. The administration reviewed statistics, the market fixed prices, and society accepted it as misfortune. Obedience became a weapon—people continued to follow rules, even when the rules themselves were the problem.

The Bengal famine also reveals that money is not merely the reward of hard work, as we are taught from childhood. History shows that money is often the product of a system—of rules designed by a few and endured by the many. For some, rules are created in such a way that they cannot lose; they possess storage, capital, and political access. For the majority, however, the rules are set so that they can only dream of winning—because the terms of the game have already been decided against them before it even begins.

Before 1789, France was submerged in a deep economic and social crisis. Bread, the staple food of the common people, kept becoming more expensive. Peasants and laborers worked tirelessly throughout the day, yet their stomachs remained half-empty. The burden of taxation fell upon them, while their incomes remained stagnant. Hunger was no longer a personal hardship; it had become a collective experience.

In stark contrast, life in royal palaces and among the aristocracy showed no signs of deprivation. Lavish banquets continued at court, storehouses remained full, and those connected to power were largely insulated from the economic crisis. This inequality was not merely about unequal resources; it was about privileges protected by the system itself. The structure of the state ensured that those at the top remained secure under all circumstances, while crisis became a permanent condition for those at the bottom.

When hunger and injustice crossed the limits of endurance, the people began to question the king and the system. These questions had not emerged overnight; they had been suppressed for centuries—questions about taxation, lack of representation, and social injustice. The French Revolution was the eruption of this long-repressed discontent. Symbols of power fell, monarchy was dismantled, and ideals such as "liberty, equality, and fraternity" came to the forefront.

But history does not end there. It soon became clear that changing the form of power does not automatically eliminate inequality. New rulers replaced kings, a new elite emerged in place of the old nobility, and economic power once again concentrated in limited hands. The system changed, but the underlying logic did not—the logic through which resources flow upward and burdens are pushed downward.

In this sense, France in 1789 is not merely a story of the past. It is part of a recurring historical pattern in which people endure until survival itself becomes impossible. And when they finally rise, power shifts—but often the same game begins again. History does not hide the truth that the problem is not only the ruler; the problem is the structure that prepares a few to always win and the majority to always endure.

In 2013, a garment factory building known as Rana Plaza, located in the Savar area of Bangladesh, collapsed. More than a thousand workers were killed and thousands more were injured. These workers stitched clothes for famous international brands—brands whose advertisements speak the language of modernity, ethics, and progress.

Investigations made it clear that the building was unsafe. Cracks had appeared in the walls. Warnings about the danger had been issued a day earlier. Factory owners were aware of all this. But halting production would have meant a disruption of profits. And so, the factory remained open the next day.

The workers, too, were aware of the danger. But they had no real choices. Going to work meant risking their lives. Not going to work meant hunger. This is the point at which calling an event an "accident" becomes dishonest to history. This was not an accident. It was a structural compromise made between greed and compulsion.

This incident exposes a global economic system in which risk is pushed downward while profit is pulled upward. The factory owners were safe. The brands were safe. The consumers were safe. The only ones unsafe were those whose hands produced the goods.

Society calls this development. It is said that factories create employment. Markets bring progress. But history asks a fundamental question—progress for whom?

If this is development, why does its burden always fall on the bodies of the poor? If the market is fair, why are those who work the hardest the cheapest?

We are taught to believe that hard work is the key to success. But Rana Plaza shows that there is no direct relationship between labor and profit. Profit is often not the result of hard work, but of power, control, and the ability to make rules. For some, rules are designed so that they remain almost free of risk; for the majority, rules are designed so that risk becomes a daily condition of life.

Rana Plaza teaches us that in the modern world, exploitation does not always arrive with whips and chains. Sometimes it arrives in the name of employment, speaks the language of development, and presents the absence of choice as "free choice." But when a human being has no option other than hunger or danger, their choice is not truly a choice—it is compulsion.

In this sense, Rana Plaza was not merely the collapse of a building. It was the collapse of the illusion that markets automatically produce justice. History repeatedly shows that unless the system itself is questioned, progress remains security for those at the top and sacrifice for those at the bottom.

That is why, in every era, laws speak of equality in books, while the picture on the streets looks entirely different. History makes it clear that poverty is not an accident. It is a condition that is allowed to continue because it keeps the system running. If everyone were satisfied, who would obey orders? If everyone were equal, who would sit at the top?

And here another question arises: if money is so powerful that it can override hunger, labor, and justice, then who controls this power?

Who decides where money flows—and where it dries up?

After 2001, laws were enacted in the United States in the name of "security" that fundamentally altered the very definition of civic life. Under legislation such as the Patriot Act, the state was granted the authority to monitor ordinary people's phone calls, emails, travel, and private activities. These freedoms were not taken away openly. People were told that liberty would be slightly reduced, but in return they would receive security.

Gradually, this abnormal condition began to feel normal. Citizens noticed their privacy shrinking, but fear ran so deep that resistance weakened. Power did not need to use force to take anything away. It merely displayed fear—and people surrendered their freedoms voluntarily. This was not the first time in history. Whenever societies have been frightened, they have handed over their freedoms as a "temporary sacrifice." And that temporary sacrifice has often become permanent.

The politics of fear finds its most extreme expression in war. In 2003, the United States and its allies launched an attack on Iraq. It was claimed that Iraq possessed weapons of mass destruction that posed a threat to the entire world. This claim was repeatedly reinforced by governments, media, and experts. Ordinary people accepted it as truth. The war was presented as moral, necessary, and defensive.

Within a few years, however, it became clear that such weapons had never existed. No concrete evidence was found. But by then it was too late. Iraqi cities had been destroyed. Infrastructure lay in ruins. Millions of ordinary civilians had been killed or displaced.

A clear pattern emerges here. Decisions about war are made in corridors of power, but their cost is paid in streets, homes, and hospitals. Those who give the orders to drop bombs remain safe. Those who die are people who neither chose the war nor shaped the policy. They were simply born there.

History repeatedly reinforces this truth: wars are never fought by those who start them, nor do those who justify them end up dying. Power portrays itself as moral. It decides who is a patriot and who is a traitor. Those who ask questions become suspicious. Those who resist are labeled dangerous. Fear is not merely an emotional reaction; it is a political instrument. Through it, obedience is manufactured. Human beings are controlled not by weapons alone, but through the language of morality, patriotism, and security. And when this control succeeds, power no longer even needs violence—people begin to believe, on their own, that its decisions are right.

In 1986, in Chernobyl, Ukraine, a nuclear power plant collapsed after a massive explosion. The project had been presented as a "victory of science" and the "future of energy." It was claimed that technology would free humanity from its limitations. Yet within a few hours, the entire region turned toxic. The air, the water, the soil—everything was contaminated.

At first, the government chose silence. Information was withheld. The danger was downplayed. By the time the truth emerged, it was already too late. Thousands had been exposed to radiation. Millions were forced to abandon their homes forever. Those who had made no policies and taken no technical decisions paid the price of an experiment with their lives.

This was not the first time that the dream of "progress" turned into punishment for ordinary people. Chernobyl reveals how the risks of technological decisions are pushed downward, while the credit flows upward. When an experiment succeeds, it is called an achievement. When it fails, it is labeled an accident.

In 1995, something similar happened in Chicago, USA—but without an explosion, without machines. That year, a devastating heat wave struck the city. In wealthy neighborhoods, air conditioners ran nonstop. In poorer areas, thousands of elderly people died. The city was the same. The weather was the same. The difference lay only in living conditions.

This was not a natural disaster. It was the outcome of social inequality. Those with resources survived. Those without them died. Yet it was recorded as a "heat wave"—as if the weather had caused the deaths, not the system.

History makes one thing clear here. Progress is rarely distributed equally, even though it is claimed in the name of everyone. Society is said to be moving forward, while in reality some move ahead and others are left behind. And the cost paid by those left behind is normalized as "collateral damage."

This pattern has not been limited to capitalist systems alone. The Soviet Union also collapsed—once described as a dream of equality and justice. Colonialism too came to an end—once justified in the name of civilization and development. Every system presented itself as the final solution. And every time, after a while, the same cracks reappeared: the concentration of power, unequal access to resources, and the use of fear.

History does not claim that all systems are identical. But it does show that power, greed, and fear return in some form within every system. The names change. The language changes. The arguments change. But the structure often remains the same.

Perhaps the most dangerous thing is not that these systems fail. The most dangerous thing is that even after witnessing these failures, human beings do not give up hope. They believe that next time everything will be different. This hope keeps society moving—and this same hope blinds it. Because in the name of hope, questions are postponed. And when questions are not asked, history begins to repeat itself.

Have you ever thought — if someone is told: forget everything — your name, nationality, identity, religion, all definitions of right and wrong — and simply say who you are, most people fall completely silent for a moment. Because all their life they have learned everything, except who they themselves are. Just think — in every school around you, don't you see the same picture every day? Hundreds of children, identical uniforms, identical lines, identical steps. No questions in their eyes, no curiosity on their faces. The bell rings and they all walk inside together, as if raw material has been pushed into a factory. No one asks what this child wants to become. They only check how "well they can fit in."

A mother tells her child, "Don't ask too many questions, people will find you strange." The mother is not bad — she was taught the same thing. She too was never taught that asking questions is not wrong, that stopping questions is actually far more dangerous. Slowly the child understands that silence is the safest place. That is where his real training begins.

One day the same child grows up and sits in some ceremony. Someone on the stage declares, "A good person is the one who follows rules." The entire hall claps. No one wonders who made those rules, why they were made, and for whose benefit. Clapping is easy; thinking is heavy. Society is clever. It doesn't put chains on people — it puts habits on them.

Then gives them names — tradition, culture, decency. And humans believe that whatever has always happened must be right. No one tells them that wrong things also travel through generations. The one who memorizes the most is called intelligent.

The one who quietly obeys is called civilized. The one who thinks differently is called lost. And eventually, even that person learns that standing apart from the crowd is rarely safe.

Just imagine in a village, a man wants to try a new method in his field. Two people laugh and say, "Our fathers and grandfathers never did this." The man falls silent — not because his method was wrong, but because the fear of being alone was bigger. That is society's greatest strength. It doesn't forbid — it frightens. Fear of being different, fear of asking questions, fear of simply being oneself. And slowly a person becomes exactly what was expected of them. They feel this was their own choice, though the habit of choosing was taken away long ago. Society wants people who work, but do not question — who obey, but do not examine. But then why does an emptiness remain inside?

Why does that restlessness rise again and again that something here is not truly mine? Perhaps because a person is never really given a chance to meet themselves without all the borrowed layers. Imagine in a courtroom stands a man. He has killed no one, robbed no one, snatched nothing from anyone. Yet he is punished — because he went against "the law." The law — which can neither be seen nor touched — yet decides someone's entire life. Our world is full of such invisible powers — religion, morality, reputation, tradition. They cannot be seen, yet they press upon life as if they were standing right in front of us.

An old man goes to the temple every day. He asks for nothing— he just folds his hands with fear, afraid something might go wrong. Society has replaced external masters with masters inside the mind. Now humans don't fear kings, they fear their own thoughts — "This is not right to think, this desire is wrong, this wish is sinful." The most dangerous rulers are those invisible ones that have been declared sacred.

From childhood, society teaches us: obey orders, do not question, breaking rules is wrong. Gradually, the mind becomes accustomed to obedience, whether the authority is speaking the truth or a lie. It is this mental framework that has, across different eras, led people to consider violence in the name of power, religion, nation, or market as a "duty."

History makes it clear that humans are won over less by the sword and more by ideas. Once the mind bends, the body follows automatically—and this is the most dangerous state, because the individual may not even realize when they have been living someone else's imposed thoughts.

This raises the question—if thought can be controlled, if opportunities are predetermined from birth, if wealth and inequality are structural—then whose interests does power truly serve?

Why Political Power Never Serves

Power is not a modern invention; it is as old as human history itself. Power emerged as soon as human beings began to live in groups. Its origin did not lie in any moral ideal, but in the need for control, protection, and command over resources. Historical inquiry makes this evident: the fundamental logic of power has never changed—only its forms have. Monarchies, empires, colonial regimes, nation-states, and democracies have differed in structure and language, yet the central objective of power has remained constant: to preserve itself.

The problem of power is therefore not merely a contemporary political debate. It has existed from the earliest phases of human civilization. To understand the origins of power, one must go far beyond the nation-state, constitutions, or modern democracy and return to prehistoric human societies. This is not simply a journey into the past but an attempt to trace the roots of present-day power structures.

In prehistoric times, human communities were primarily hunter–gatherers—small, mobile groups whose survival depended directly on nature. In this phase, power was not formalized. There were no permanent rulers and no institutionalized governance. Decisions were largely collective, shaped by the necessities of cooperation for survival. Food, shelter, and security demanded the participation of the entire group.

In these societies, resource accumulation was practically impossible. Food was perishable, and land was not privately owned. As a result, social inequality remained limited. Leadership was temporary and situational—one person might guide the hunt, another might lead during crises. Such leadership was responsibility rather than domination.

Anthropological studies indicate that such societies were characterized by: Decision-making through consensus, social discouragement of excessive dominance, the practical impossibility of centralized authority. There could be no permanent structure of power because the material and social conditions necessary to sustain it did not yet exist.

A decisive transformation occurred with the development of agriculture. Farming led to permanent settlement, and permanent settlement made resource accumulation possible. Land, grain, and livestock ceased to be transient and became storable and controllable property. Here we see the real birth of enduring power.

Agriculture produced three fundamental changes: 1. the creation of surplus 2. the possibility of private control 3. the emergence of social stratification.

Those who controlled more land possessed more grain, and those who possessed more grain could impose dependence on others. Dependence generated control, and control crystallized into power. This was not the outcome of any conspiracy; it was a structural inevitability. Once resources became both limited and accumulable, mechanisms for their regulation became necessary—and wherever regulation appears, inequality follows.

In agricultural societies, social roles slowly differentiated: Some people produced, some defended, some administered.

From here, class structure developed. The producing class—primarily cultivators—gradually became subordinate, while administrative and military classes rose to dominance. Power now began to shift from personal influence to institutional organization.

This power was not grounded solely in physical force. As societies grew more complex, power required legitimacy—a justification placed beyond ordinary questioning. Early states in Mesopotamia, ancient Egypt, and the Indus Valley tied political authority to divine sanction. The king was not merely a ruler; he was proclaimed the representative—or embodiment—of the gods. This association marked a decisive turning point.

Divine legitimacy achieved three things:

1. it insulated power from moral scrutiny.
2. it presented inequality as natural and inevitable.
3. it redefined dissent as sin or sacrilege.

Opposition to power thus became not only a political offense but a religious transgression. To suppress criticism, brute force alone was no longer required; faith sufficed. In Mesopotamia, one finds the earliest written legal codes—such as the Code of Hammurabi—declared to be of divine origin. The king did not claim to make law; he claimed merely to transmit divine will. Law thereby ceased to be a tool to question power and became a means to protect it. These codes did not enforce equality; they enforced hierarchical control, prescribing different punishments for different social strata and presenting such inequality as divinely ordained.

In ancient Egypt, the pharaoh was regarded as a god in human form. Power and religion were completely fused. Challenging the pharaoh was equated with disturbing the cosmic order (Ma'at). In this structure: Labor belonged to the people, monuments belonged to power, glory belonged to the god-king. The pyramids were not only architectural achievements; they were permanent symbols of power—designed to announce that power was not mortal but eternal.

The Indus Valley civilization appears somewhat different, with less evidence of personal kingship or monumental palaces. This does not indicate the absence of power, but rather the presence of power in a more administrative and impersonal form. Planned cities, standardized bricks, and sophisticated water systems imply central coordination and control, even if less overtly sacralized. Across these cases, a clear historical pattern emerges:

resources → control

control → power

power → legitimacy

legitimacy → acceptance of inequality

Power has rarely presented itself as force alone. It has consistently appeared as god, tradition, law, or order—while its foundational purpose has remained the same: its own preservation.

In modern political discourse, ancient Greece—particularly Athens—is frequently celebrated as the birthplace of democracy. Textbooks, university curricula, and political speeches repeatedly claim that it was in Greece that ordinary people first gained participation in political power. Yet this claim, though popular, is profoundly incomplete and misleading.

A careful and critical examination of the political structures of ancient Greece reveals that Athenian "democracy" was neither universal nor inclusive, nor was it an honest attempt to place power in the hands of the entire populace. Rather, Greek democracy represents not a moral transformation of power but a strategic reconfiguration of it.

To begin with, ancient Greece was not a unified nation. It consisted of hundreds of city-states (polis)—Athens, Sparta, Corinth, Thebes, and many others—each with its own systems of governance, social arrangements, and power relations. "Greek democracy," therefore, was not a single uniform model but a cluster of diverse experiments in the exercise of power. Athens receives special prominence primarily because a system of direct democracy developed there. However, the crucial question is: democracy for whom? When examined on its actual social foundations, Athenian democracy appears as a form of restricted democracy. It was not based on universal rights but on a narrowly defined conception of citizenship. Who counted as a citizen? In Athens, a citizen was only one who:

1. was a free male.
2. was born in Athens.
3. had both parents of Athenian origin.

Who was excluded? By this definition, the following were entirely excluded from political life: women, slaves, resident foreigners (metics).

Historians estimate that nearly 80–85 percent of the total population of Athens was excluded from democratic participation. Thus, the democracy so often praised was confined to a small minority.

It is often assumed that democracy in Athens emerged to transfer power from rulers to "the people." Historical analysis, however, suggests a different purpose. Athenian democracy evolved out of conflicts between:

The aristocratic elite, and the emerging middle groups such as merchants and soldiers. Democracy did not abolish power; it reorganized it. Power ceased to be concentrated solely in a few noble families and was instead shared among a broader—but still privileged—citizen class. Even this sharing remained limited to those already endowed with status and advantage.

In this sense, democracy in Athens was: not a project to empower the entire populace, but a mechanism to maintain balance within the ruling classes themselves. Democracy made power more invisible and legitimate, not necessarily more just.

Athenian citizens participated directly in the popular assembly (Ecclesia), unlike in modern representative democracies. However, this "directness" is frequently romanticized. In practice: Regular participation was only feasible for those with leisure and economic security, poorer citizens had limited presence, rhetorical skill became a crucial instrument of power.

Thus democracy transformed speech and persuasion into tools of dominance; those who spoke better wielded greater influence.

Moreover, Athenian democracy was structurally dependent on slavery. The number of slaves exceeded that of citizens. Citizens could devote time to political affairs precisely because: Slaves performed the essential labor, and women managed domestic responsibilities.

The entire democratic framework, therefore, rested upon an undemocratic social foundation. Without slavery, this democratic system could not have functioned. This fact profoundly undercuts the moral prestige often attached to Athenian democracy.

If Athens represents the restricted experiment of democracy, Sparta illustrates another form of power—military oligarchy. In Sparta: power was concentrated in a few militarized families, the purpose of life was not individual well-being but the strength of the state, obedience constituted the highest virtue.

The entire life of citizens was organized around: training, discipline, warfare. Sparta too rested on the exploitation of slaves (Helots), whose labor sustained the military state.

Ancient Greek democracy, then, was not an ideal model but a historically specific experiment marked by clear limitations. Presenting it uncritically as the pure origin of democracy in contemporary political discourse is not only intellectually careless but historically inaccurate.

Rome is one of the most precise and instructive examples for understanding the true nature of power. Like ancient Greece, Rome is often associated with democratic ideals, especially because of its early Republican period. However, a closer study of Roman history makes it clear that the transition from Republic to Empire was not the result of some sudden moral decline or accidental slide into tyranny. This transition was the natural outcome of the internal logic of power and the structural pressures built into the Roman system itself.

Rome demonstrates that power tolerates democratic processes only so long as they do not obstruct its expansion and stability. The moment such processes become inconvenient, they are neutralized or abolished.

The Roman Republic was established in 509 BCE after the fall of the monarchy. In principle, it was a system based on citizen participation, the rule of law, and institutional balance. The Senate, popular assemblies, and elected magistrates together created the appearance of democratic governance.

In practice, however, real power remained concentrated in the hands of a small number of aristocratic families—the Patricians. The Senate, the most powerful institution in the Republic, was firmly controlled by this elite. The participation of ordinary citizens, the Plebeians, was limited; their political power was more symbolic than substantive. Here an important fact becomes evident:

In the Roman Republic, democracy was not the source of power; it was the instrument through which power claimed legitimacy. For a long period, the Roman social order was marked by conflict between Patricians and Plebeians. This struggle produced certain reforms—greater representation for Plebeians, some legal rights, and the office of the Tribune. Yet these reforms did not alter the fundamental structure of power.

They were not introduced to challenge power, but to contain social unrest. This reflects an old political strategy: stabilizing deep inequality through limited concessions. The decisive turning point in Rome came with its military expansion. As Rome extended beyond Italy, war became a permanent condition. With continuous warfare came three major changes:

1. the army ceased to be a temporary citizen militia,
2. soldiers became economically dependent on war,
3. generals emerged as immensely powerful figures.

Loyalty slowly shifted from the state to individual commanders because: salaries, grants of land, and personal protection were provided not by the Senate but by the generals themselves. The center of power thus began moving away from institutions toward individuals. During this period, commanders such as Marius, Sulla, and ultimately Julius Caesar became extraordinarily influential. They gained support from both the army and the masses—not because of democratic ideals, but because of: economic inequality, land crises, and widespread unemployment. Generals promised relief, and in return, the populace became willing to accept the concentration of power. This reveals a crucial truth:

When institutions fail to solve people's problems, people begin to accept centralized authority. Julius Caesar is often portrayed as the destroyer of the Republic, but this interpretation is incomplete. Caesar was not merely the cause; he was also the symptom of the Republic's collapse.

He: Ignored the Senate, seized power through military strength, and declared himself "dictator for life. Yet this was possible only because: Republican institutions had become ineffective, the Senate had grown detached from the people, and power now demanded stability, not debate.

Even Caesar's assassination failed to revive the Republic, because the root problem was structural rather than personal. After Caesar, Octavian—later Augustus—took control. Instead of open dictatorship, he adopted a far subtler strategy. Augustus: preserved the outward forms of the Republic, but concentrated real power in his own hands, and called himself "first citizen" (Princeps) rather than king. This represented a refined form of rule—dictatorship without the title of dictator.

Republican institutions continued to exist formally, but the power to make decisions rested with the emperor. The Roman Empire employed a simple yet remarkably effective strategy to render the populace politically passive—"bread and circuses."

Through: The distribution of free grain, lavish public spectacles, and gladiatorial games, the aim was not social justice or equality. Rather, these policies were designed to: keep the masses preoccupied, create an appearance of contentment, and divert attention away from political questions and power structures.

In this way, material provision and entertainment functioned as instruments of political management. Public welfare was not pursued as a right of citizens but as a tool to secure obedience and discourage critical engagement with authority.

"Panem et circenses"

— "Give them bread and circuses, and they will never revolt"

— Juvenal (Roman satirist, circa 1st–2nd century CE)

— Juvenal wrote this sentence in his satirical work Satires

Medieval history is frequently portrayed as an "age of faith"—a period supposedly governed by God, religion, and morality. This portrayal, however, is a simplification. In reality, the medieval period was not the age of religion itself, but the age of the political use of religion. It was during this era that ruling elites clearly recognized that long-term governance could not rest solely on force or military power. Power required stability, and stability demanded a form of legitimacy that would stand beyond questioning. Religion became the most effective source of such legitimacy.

In the medieval world, religion did not function as an alternative to political authority; rather, it served as its supporting instrument. Churches, mosques, monasteries, and temples operated less as institutions restraining power and more as mechanisms for disciplining the populace.

In medieval Europe, political authority rested on a close alliance between the Church and the monarchy. This alliance was not the outcome of spiritual consensus, but of mutual advantage. Kings ruled, and the Church sanctified their rule.

(a) The doctrine of the Divine Right of Kings

Across Europe, the claim was widely propagated that kings ruled by the will of God. This doctrine rendered criticism of political power virtually impossible. If the king was appointed by God, then: questioning his commands, criticizing his decisions, or rebelling against him was equated with rebellion against God himself. Political dissent was thus transformed into religious crime.

(b) The role of the Church: not morality, but legitimacy

The Church presented itself as a moral institution, yet in practice it acted as the principal manufacturer of political legitimacy. It: crowned kings, declared wars to be "holy," and branded opponents of power as heretics. Whoever resisted authority became not only a traitor to the crown but also an enemy of God. Religion here served not the spiritual elevation of the people, but the imposition of political discipline.

Religion in medieval Europe functioned not only as a source of legitimacy but also as an instrument of intellectual control. The Church claimed the authority to define: What counted as truth, what constituted knowledge, and what was sin. Ideas incompatible with established power were condemned as heresy. Scientists, philosophers, and social critics were frequently targeted by ecclesiastical courts. Religion thus:

Regulated knowledge, criminalized questioning, and portrayed existing power structures as immutable. It becomes evident that the primary function of religion in medieval Europe was not to disseminate morality, but to consolidate power. In China, rulers relied less on organized religion and more on tradition and moral philosophy. The doctrine of the "Mandate of Heaven" asserted that the sovereign ruled by celestial sanction. This concept: Endowed power with moral legitimacy, naturalized social inequality, and framed rebellion as a moral disorder. Here too, power operated not for the service of the people, but for the benefit of: The court, the military, and the administrative elite. Whether in Europe or China, the same structural pattern emerges:

Power seeks permanence, permanence requires legitimacy, and legitimacy is most effectively secured through religion, tradition, or culture. Religion, in this process: Freed power from ethical scrutiny, shielded it from criticism, and subordinated the populace psychologically.

At the same time, religion itself became dependent upon power. In medieval empires, governance was rarely designed for the welfare of ordinary people. The real beneficiaries were the court, the army, and the nobility. Ordinary people paid taxes, provided labor, fought wars, and in return received religious sermons and moral injunctions. Religion served to justify exploitation.

Medieval history therefore demonstrates that religion was not the antagonist of power, but its most reliable ally. It furnished power with: a moral façade, protection from critique, and the sanctification of inequality. Power always arms itself with an ideology—sometimes religion, sometimes tradition, sometimes culture. The forms change; the logic does not.

The British Empire is often portrayed in modern history through two extreme lenses. On the one hand, it is celebrated as a force that brought "civilization, law, and modernity." On the other, it is depicted as entirely exploitative, brutal, and destructive. The historical reality lies between these extremes. No political power is entirely benevolent or wholly malevolent. However, this balanced view should not obscure a fundamental fact: the primary objective of the British Empire was not the welfare of the colonies, but the expansion and preservation of imperial power.

The British Empire represented a modern form of power in which military force was combined with administration, law, education, and ideology as instruments of control. This was a form of colonialism that did not simply present itself as a violent conqueror; it carefully crafted the image of a "civilizing guardian."

The ideological framework through which Britain justified its rule across India, Africa, Asia, and other regions was both sophisticated and strategically significant. Colonial domination was legitimized through three principal claims: first, that it was bringing civilization; second, that it was establishing law and order; and third, that it was providing modern education and administration. These narratives endowed colonialism with a veneer of moral authority, portraying power not as exploitative but as redemptive, a force that uplifted the supposedly "backward" societies under imperial guidance. This ideological positioning constituted one of the most effective and enduring successes of colonial rule, enabling the empire to maintain control while projecting an image of benevolence. Yet, beneath this moralistic rhetoric lay extensive coercion, relentless economic extraction, and widespread human suffering—realities that the ideological framing could not erase and that remain central to understanding the profound costs of colonialism.

The British Empire was therefore neither purely civilizing nor purely barbaric. It was a highly organized structure of power that employed the language of modernity to institutionalize control.

The twentieth century is frequently described as the "democratic turn" in human history. Empires declined, colonialism weakened, and nation-states emerged. During this period, it was widely proclaimed that power had finally passed into the hands of the people. Kings, emperors, and colonial rulers disappeared, replaced by constitutions, parliaments, and elections. In theory, this shift was interpreted as a moral evolution of political power.

However, a closer examination of the functioning of the nation-state and modern democracy reveals that the basic logic of power did not fundamentally change. What changed was its form, language, and technology. Modern democracy does not abolish power; it renders power more refined, more acceptable, and often more invisible.

The emergence of the nation-state was closely connected with the decline of empires. After the First and Second World Wars, the idea gained strength that power should belong not to a dynasty or empire, but to the "nation." The nation was presented as a shared identity, a common history, and a collective destiny. This was a powerful idea because it relocated power from an external ruler into the imagined community of "us."

Yet this raises a fundamental question: who exactly constitutes this "we"? Nation-states declared all citizens equal in law, yet economic, social, and political power remained deeply unequal. Power was no longer concentrated in the hands of a king; it became concentrated within: state institutions, bureaucratic systems, and military-administrative apparatuses. Empires collapsed, but the structures of domination did not. Democracy is often described as "rule by the people." In practice, however, the role of citizens in modern democracies largely consists of: Voting, choosing representatives, and then waiting for the next election.

Real power over: Policy formation, distribution of resources, and major decision-making rarely lies in the hands of the populace. Democracy thus becomes less a mechanism for the transfer of power, and more an instrument for the management of power. Elections change governments; they seldom change power structures.

In modern nation-states, power operates through a coalition of institutions—political parties, economic capital, and the media.

(a) Political parties:

Political parties claim to represent the people, but in practice they primarily function as: organizations seeking power whose fundamental aim is to retain power. Their policies are often shaped less by public need and more by: Electoral arithmetic, donors, and corporate interests.

(b) The role of capital:

In modern democracies, economic power readily transforms into political power. Elections are expensive, campaigns require financing, and policymaking is influenced by corporate pressures. Thus: Everyone votes, but only a few exercise disproportionate influence. This is one of democracy's silent contradictions.

(c) Media: information or the manufacture of consent?

The media is often described as the "fourth pillar" of democracy. In reality, contemporary media is frequently: Not independent of power, but closely intertwined with political and economic interests. Its role increasingly shifts from providing information to manufacturing consent. Modern power relies less on overt coercion and more on persuasion, narrative-building, and emotional mobilization. Violence becomes less visible; it operates through language, symbols, and images.

Power today: Presents itself as "national interest," labels criticism as disloyalty, and portrays dissent as a threat. This represents a highly sophisticated form of authority—one in which citizens themselves become defenders of the very power that governs them.

Modern democracies extensively deploy identity politics. Nation, religion, caste, ethnicity, and language become emotional resources for power. When: Economic inequality deepens and social problems remain unresolved, attention is diverted from material issues toward identity-based conflicts. Citizens cease to function as critical participants and are transformed into members of mobilized identity groups. Power then stabilizes itself by arbitrating among these groups and presenting itself as indispensable.

Formally, dissent is permitted in modern democracies, but in practice it is often contained and delegitimized. Protest is labeled disorder; questioning is branded anti-national; critics are portrayed as enemies of the state. This process morally sanctifies power while dehumanizing opposition. Democracy becomes less about the freedom to ask questions and more about the regulation of which questions may be asked.

The distinguishing feature of modern democracy is not the absence of power, but the subtlety with which it operates. It uses less overt violence, presents itself as the will of the people, and functions through systems of consent rather than fear. This does not make it inherently more ethical; it simply makes it: More efficient, more psychological, and more widely accepted.

Nation-states and democracies therefore do not signal the end of power; they represent its modern incarnation. Kings disappeared, empires dissolved—yet control, hierarchy, and domination persisted in new and more sophisticated forms. Political power is among the most frequently used yet least clearly defined concepts in political discourse. It is commonly presented in the language of governance, leadership, public service, or the *"will of the people."* In democratic systems, political power is said to derive legitimacy from elections, while in authoritarian systems it is justified in the name of stability, security, or national interest.

However, all these presentations share a fundamental limitation: they obscure the structural nature of political power. This chapter challenges the assumption that the primary purpose of political power is public welfare. On the contrary, it argues that political power is fundamentally a mechanism for maintaining control over society and for reproducing itself across time.

From an academic standpoint, political power cannot be understood merely as influence or leadership. It goes beyond influence and concerns the capacity to make binding decisions and to ensure their implementation. Political power may therefore be defined as:

"Political power is the institutional capacity through which a limited segment of society determines the conditions of life, access to resources, and patterns of behavior of the majority, while simultaneously producing legitimacy for this control."

Political power can be understood as a structured phenomenon resting on three core elements: the centralization of decision-making, the structural inequality between rulers and the ruled, and the processes through which legitimacy is formed. This conceptualization draws on Max Weber's theory of authority, Michel Foucault's analysis of power–knowledge relations, and Noam Chomsky's notion of "manufactured consent." In democratic societies, political power is often conflated with leadership and service: leadership is assumed to arise from voluntary following, and service implies prioritizing the welfare of others. However, political power, by contrast, operates independently of moral virtue, can function even in the absence of consent, and retains ultimate authority to employ coercion and punitive measures. To equate political power with service or ethical leadership is therefore analytically misleading. Individuals occupying positions of authority may be personally honest or well-intentioned, yet the structure of power compels them to maintain the very arrangements from which their authority derives.

Political power manifests through two primary mechanisms: coercion and the manufacture of consent. Coercion is the direct and visible form of power and encompasses policing, military force, punitive legal frameworks, and surveillance mechanisms. Even in established democracies such as India, coercive instruments remain operational: colonial-era provisions like sedition laws and contemporary legislation such as the Unlawful

Activities (Prevention) Act demonstrate that the exceptional coercive capacities of the state persist, despite the democratic institutional façade. In comparison, consent is both more effective and less costly, and modern states rely heavily on its manufacture. The principal instruments for generating consent include elections, nationalism, religion, and media and propaganda.

Elections in India are widely celebrated as symbols of popular participation, yet they do not fundamentally challenge the structure of power; instead, they renew its legitimacy. Democracy, popularly imagined as "rule of the people," functions in practice as a system for managing authority. Electoral processes do not alter the underlying logic of governance; they simply legitimize the governing elite at regular intervals. In the Indian context, economic and educational inequalities remain stark, media and corporate capital exert decisive influence, and policy continuity persists regardless of the party in office. Democracy humanizes power in appearance without dissolving it in substance.

Political and economic power are deeply intertwined. State policies often reinforce economic structures that sustain political authority, visible in the alignment of corporate and state interests, the framing of privatization as development, and the use of welfare schemes to manage social discontent. This dynamic reflects Karl Marx's understanding of the state as a guardian of dominant class interests. Nationalism emerges as one of the most potent ideological instruments of political power, equating the state with the nation and reframing criticism of authority as hostility toward the nation itself. In India, nationalism is frequently deployed to criminalize dissent, marginalize minority communities, and restrict rights in the name of security.

The primary objectives of political power, therefore, are not service or emancipation but the self-preservation of the authority, the stability of the power structure, and the neutralization of potential challenges. These outcomes are structural realities rather than mere consequences of individual moral failure. India is not an exception; across democracies, dictatorships, and so-called socialist states, similar patterns recur: centralization of authority, restriction of dissent, and systematic production of legitimacy. Political power should neither be romanticized through idealistic lenses nor reduced to the narrow discourse of corruption. It is best understood as a structural arrangement grounded in control, legitimacy, and compliance.

Political power does not exist to serve others; it exists primarily for its own preservation. This is not a moral claim but an observable political pattern. Across history and across regimes, power behaves less like an ethical institution and more like a survival organism. Its first instinct is continuity. Service occurs only when it supports that instinct. The fundamental principle of politics is therefore simple: maintain power. All other considerations—morality, ideology, nationalism, religion, or public service—are instrumental. They are adopted when useful and abandoned when inconvenient. Political language changes with time; political incentives do not.

Leaders do not require the support of the masses. Instead, they depend on a small, decisive group whose loyalty keeps them in office. Political scientists such as Bruce Bueno de Mesquita describe this through selectorate theory: every political system contains a *"winning coalition,"* and power survives only by keeping that coalition satisfied. Whether a regime is democratic or authoritarian, the logic remains identical. Reward those few who matter, ignore those who do not.

We are conditioned to believe that politics revolves around trust, service, and ideology. Citizens are taught that leaders govern on behalf of society and that elections reflect collective will. In reality, politics is governed by arithmetic rather than ethics. How many individuals are necessary to secure authority? How many must be rewarded, intimidated, or neutralized? How much dissent can be tolerated before it becomes dangerous? This calculation—not moral intention—is the true language of power.

The greatest deception in politics is the belief that leaders serve the population as a whole. In practice, they serve only the coalition whose allegiance sustains them. Whether a system labels itself democratic or authoritarian is secondary. What matters is coalition management. Maintain loyalty through money, privilege, legal immunity, or fear, and power remains secure. Lose that loyalty, and removal becomes inevitable.

This explains why governments consistently prioritize elite interests over public welfare. Broad investments in education, healthcare, and equality reduce dependence on authority and empower citizens to question power. Such empowerment threatens political survival. Inequality, by contrast, creates dependency. Concentrated wealth and privilege guarantee loyalty. Inequality is not a governance failure; it is often a governance strategy.

Illusion plays a central role. Promises of reform, symbolic welfare schemes, subsidized essentials, and patriotic narratives pacify populations without redistributing power. Hope is carefully administered—sufficient to prevent revolt, insufficient to produce transformation. Genuine change would require transferring power away from elites, and no ruler willingly dismantles the foundations of their own authority.

Money functions as the bloodstream of political power. Instead of flowing primarily into public goods, it circulates through networks of loyal officials, financiers, security forces, and intermediaries. These actors do not support power out of belief;

they support it because their survival depends on it. Institutional decay under such systems is not accidental incompetence but deliberate design.

Resource-rich states illustrate this clearly. Oil monarchies in the Gulf depend on natural resource revenue rather than taxation. Because rulers do not rely on citizens for revenue, citizens possess little leverage. Accountability collapses. Venezuela's economic breakdown further demonstrates how resource wealth sustains elite networks while hospitals, infrastructure, and public services deteriorate. Popular suffering becomes irrelevant so long as the coalition remains funded.

Corruption is therefore not a deviation from power; it is one of its core mechanisms. No leader can reward every supporter through legitimate means alone. Illicit access becomes the substitute. Bureaucrats extract bribes, contractors inflate tenders, and ministers profit from opaque systems. Such behavior is not merely tolerated—it is structurally encouraged. Corruption binds elites together through shared risk and shared benefit. Integrity threatens power; corruption stabilizes it.

In Nigeria, billions in oil revenues have vanished into private hands while public infrastructure collapses. In India, inflated infrastructure projects enrich contractors and political elites while delivering substandard outcomes. Corruption ensures loyalty by making defection costly and honesty dangerous.

The size of the ruling coalition may differ, but the principle remains constant. A dictator may require the loyalty of a few dozen individuals; a democratic leader may require millions of votes. Smaller coalitions demand higher individual rewards; larger coalitions require broader but still selective distribution. In every case, power rests not with those who believe in ideals, but with those whose allegiance can be secured. Those excluded from this circle are ignored, marginalized, or silenced. Political relevance is determined not by justice, but by utility.

This logic explains why leaders who genuinely attempt to serve public interest rarely survive. Redirecting resources toward society weakens elite loyalty. Coalitions fracture. Removal follows. Mohammad Mossadegh of Iran, who sought to nationalize oil for public benefit, was overthrown within two years. Politics operates not on virtue, but on incentives. Policies that harm society may strengthen rulers; policies that benefit society may threaten them.

Money alone is insufficient. Power also relies on fear and manufactured consent. As Noam Chomsky explains, modern systems rarely depend on overt repression alone. Instead, they shape perception. Media systems, political discourse, and public debate limit what can be questioned. People are not silenced; they are conditioned. Obedience becomes voluntary because alternatives are rendered unthinkable.

Fear suppresses dissent and disciplines the press. In North Korea, truth itself is fatal. In Russia, journalists exposing corruption face imprisonment or death. Even within democracies, whistleblowers are punished while corrupt officials remain protected. Fear narrows thought and redirects attention away from structural injustice.

Education and healthcare are therefore systematically weakened. An educated population questions authority; questioning threatens power. Under Taliban rule, girls are denied education precisely because knowledge undermines control. Hunger becomes another weapon. In Zimbabwe, food aid has been distributed selectively to regime supporters. A population fighting for survival lacks the capacity to organize for freedom.

Foreign aid often reinforces these dynamics. Loans and grants rarely reach ordinary citizens. They strengthen military forces, surveillance systems, and elite privilege. Billions in aid to Egypt after 2011 fortified military rule while producing little improvement in daily life. When rulers depend on foreign capital rather than domestic taxation, accountability disappears. Consent is replaced by dependency.

Democracy is not immune to this logic. In practice, it often mirrors dictatorship. Power does not reside with the electorate as a whole, but with those who control pathways to victory: corporate lobbies in the United States, caste blocs in India, media oligarchs elsewhere. Leaders do not require universal approval—only a winning margin. Once elected, they govern primarily for those who secured that margin.

Democracy thus becomes a mask. Beneath it operates the same survival logic found in authoritarian regimes. Institutions differ; incentives do not. Protect the coalition. Reward loyalty. Marginalize the rest. The greatest weapon of a dictator is the innocence of the people. The greatest threat to power is their awareness.

India's system of governance appears democratic, but its underlying logic is not. Elections, parliaments, courts, and the media all exist, yet their primary function is not to empower citizens but to legitimize power. Authority does not rest on the broad consent of the people; rather, it depends on a narrow and decisive coalition. This coalition may change over time, but its fundamental nature remains constant. For those who hold power, what society wants is less important than who can preserve the existing structure of rule.

Democracy sustains the illusion that every citizen possesses equal political power. In reality, political influence is unequally distributed. Certain groups shape policy, while the majority merely live with its consequences. For power, the value of the public lies not in its numbers but in its utility. Those who can supply resources, legitimacy, stability, or control become politically relevant; the rest are managed through emotional appeals, symbolic programs, and promises.

Money is the central axis of this system, because modern power is driven not by ideas or morality, but by the flow of resources. Policy follows the direction in which money moves, and wherever policy goes, the future is shaped. The belief that public resources are primarily used for the welfare of citizens is one of power's most successful myths. In reality, a substantial portion of these resources is spent on maintaining mechanisms that ensure the continuity of rule. This expenditure is often invisible—sometimes in the name of security, sometimes development, sometimes stability—but its purpose remains clear: to create a safe environment for power itself.

Decisions are not taken on the basis of what will empower society in the long term, but on what will shield those in power from immediate challenges. As a result, sectors such as education and healthcare—which can cultivate independent thinking, critical capacity, and self-reliance—remain persistently neglected. Investment in these areas poses a risk to power because educated and healthy citizens do not remain merely consumers or voters; they become questioners, comparers, and demanders of accountability. Such citizens are not required by power.

In contrast, expenditures that strengthen control, propaganda, and loyalty are prioritized. Control is not limited to the use of force; it is also exercised through bureaucratic complexity, legal procedures, and economic dependence. Propaganda is not simply the dissemination of information; it is the determination of which information will be considered normal and which will be rendered abnormal. Loyalty is not just support; it is dependence—such dependence that an individual or group cannot imagine its existence without the ruling structure.

When public money is used in this way, inequality ceases to be an accident and becomes a strategy. In a highly unequal society, people struggle against each other rather than questioning those above. Poverty and insecurity are useful to power because they keep people preoccupied with immediate necessities. When life becomes a struggle for survival, ideas begin to look like luxuries. That is why the full and equal distribution of basic services is often postponed indefinitely.

Education is frequently reduced to degrees and skills. Critical thinking, the complexity of history, the structure of power, and the functioning of economic systems are systematically pushed out of curricula. Education is converted from a medium of questioning into a tool of adaptation. Similarly, healthcare is transformed from a right into a service—one whose availability depends on money, identity, and connections. An unhealthy society is rarely in a position to challenge authority.

The flow of money also determines which issues become national priorities and which are framed as individual failures. Unemployment is presented not as a structural problem but as personal inadequacy. Malnutrition is attributed not to policy failure but to cultural habits. In this way, power detaches itself from the consequences of its own decisions.

Power-aligned networks—administrative, economic, or ideological—are nourished by this financial system. Inclusion within these networks provides security; exclusion brings risk. This is why values such as honesty, transparency, and independence struggle to become institutional norms. They remain personal virtues that the structure routinely penalizes. Those who adapt to the system receive opportunities, protection, and visibility; those who do not are rendered invisible or suspicious.

This system presents itself in the language of democracy. Budgets, schemes, and announcements create the impression that resources are being allocated for the people. But allocation and impact are not the same. What appears equal on paper becomes selective in practice. This selectivity is concealed behind technical vocabulary, statistics, and procedures, making questioning itself difficult.

Through money, power controls not only the present but also confines the future. When education and healthcare are underfunded, future generations remain trapped in the same dependence. It becomes a self-sustaining cycle—low investment, low empowerment, low resistance. Breaking this cycle is not in the interest of those who benefit from it.

In such a system, the language of reform is heard often, but the definition of reform remains narrow. Reform tends to mean making existing processes more efficient rather than changing the underlying structure. Efficient inequality is acceptable to power; equality is not. Hence technology is readily embraced, but rights are not. Digital systems make control easier, but they do not necessarily expand freedom.

The centrality of money also makes it clear that power does not change through moral appeals. As long as the direction of resource flows remains the same, outcomes also remain the same. The most dangerous question for power is not whether it is moral, but whether it is necessary. When citizens begin to feel organized, educated, and secure without dependency on power, its legitimacy begins to erode.

Real change, therefore, does not come merely from changing leaders but from changing the direction of money. And this is the most difficult transformation, because it challenges the core machinery of power. Power is not afraid of service; it is afraid of freedom. And the path to freedom runs through education, healthcare, and economic security—precisely those areas that are deliberately kept weak.

Thus, money does not remain merely an economic tool; it becomes the language of power. Those who understand this language understand politics. The rest simply live within its consequences.

The media in this process is not merely a channel of communication; it becomes a central instrument of power. On the surface it appears free, diverse, and vibrant—countless channels, newspapers, websites, panel discussions, and social platforms create the impression that society is saturated with information. Yet an abundance of information is not the same as knowledge. In reality, this flood of information often drowns understanding. The number of questions increases, but their significance steadily declines. The questions that could expose the structure of power, the distribution of economic strength, and the real processes of policy formation are systematically absent.

This absence is not accidental. It is not created through open censorship, but through selection. Some issues are shown repeatedly, some are presented in a limited manner, and some disappear entirely. The viewer cannot see what is being withheld, and that constitutes the greatest success of this system. What is shown becomes "reality."

Debates happen, but they are controlled. Questions are asked, but they remain within safe boundaries. Discussions are designed to evoke emotional reactions without producing intellectual discomfort. Anger is stimulated, but thought is not. Issues are reduced to personalities, events, or symbols so that structural causes are never examined. As a result, people continue fighting the symptoms of problems but rarely reach their roots.

Emotional issues are the most effective weapon in this mechanism. Feelings of fear, pride, humiliation, and identity are repeatedly invoked. When society is trapped in emotion, it does not analyze. Emotional frenzy disables reason, and as soon as reason weakens, power becomes secure. Media directs this emotional energy—who to be angry at, whom to fear, what to be proud of is all carefully shaped.

Identity-based conflicts deepen this process further. Society is fragmented into groups whose concerns clash with one another. When people remain busy defending their identities, they do not question power. A divided society does not become a threat to authority. The media presents these divisions not as constructed but as natural, permanent, and inevitable, as if conflict were the essential condition of social existence.

Nationalist symbols provide moral cover for this entire arrangement. Decisions of those in power are framed as being in the "national interest," and anyone who questions them is viewed with suspicion. Thus criticism is transformed from dissent into betrayal. The media here does not merely mediate; it adjudicates—deciding who is legitimate and who is suspect.

Discussion of structural inequality remains absent because it touches the core question of power. If one asks why resources are so unequally distributed, or why policymaking serves a limited set of interests, the entire political–economic framework is challenged. To avoid such questions, the media redirects attention toward superficial issues—immediate, emotional, and sensational topics.

The concentration of economic power is portrayed as normal, natural, and unavoidable. It is wrapped in the language of "development," "competition," and "efficiency." The media does not ask for whom development occurs, who is excluded by competition, or who benefits from efficiency. Instead, it highlights individual success stories so that structural barriers remain invisible.

Policy-making is presented as highly technical and complex, beyond the reach of ordinary citizens. The impression is created that such decisions belong to experts rather than the public. Citizens are thus distanced from decision-making, even as they bear its consequences. Instead of bridging this gap, the media legitimizes it.

This entire process rests on the assumption that citizens do not need to know everything—they only need to know enough to react, not to intervene. Information is packaged in ways that encourage passivity. People know but do not understand; they see but cannot connect.

Social media has not weakened this system; it has made it more intricate. Information spreads faster, but its lifespan becomes shorter. One issue immediately replaces another. Constant stimulation makes depth impossible. Attention turns into a scarce resource, and whoever controls attention controls public discourse.

In such an environment, the boundary between truth and falsehood becomes blurred. Every fact is turned into an opinion, and every opinion is granted equal weight. This does not democratize knowledge; it democratizes confusion. The media legitimizes this confusion in the name of "balance" or "both sides," even when power relations are already deeply unequal.

Thus, the media does not function as an adversary of power, but as its structural ally. This collaboration is not always overt, yet its impact is profound. Power requires public consent, and the media becomes the factory where that consent is manufactured.

This consent is produced not through reason but through habit. What is seen repeatedly comes to feel true.

Ultimately, the problem is not simply that the media lies. The deeper issue is that it decides which parts of the truth will be shown and which will remain unseen. This act of selection is the real weapon of power. When society comes to believe that what is visible is the whole truth, repression becomes unnecessary.

In this sense, the greatest strength of the media is its invisibility. It presents itself as a mere mirror, whereas in reality it is the frame. And until that frame itself is questioned, society will continue mistaking curated reality for reality itself.

To protect power, no weapon, law, or army is as effective as this: the control of attention, the selection of questions, and the management of emotions. Once this process becomes normalized, repression is no longer required—people begin to defend the very system that weakens them.

Identity—whether based on caste, religion, language, or nation—is not merely a social characteristic; it is a powerful political instrument. Power does not rely primarily on overt violence or coercion to preserve itself; it depends more on the lines of division drawn within society. When society comes together around shared purposes and common questions, it becomes a challenge to authority. Conversely, when it is fragmented into identity-based compartments, it remains entangled within itself, while power stands above it, secure and unchallenged.

The political use of identity creates the illusion that the source of conflict lies within society rather than in the structure of power itself. Once people begin to believe that the root of their problems is another community, language, caste, or ideology, they stop paying attention to the policies and decisions that actually shape their lives. Through this process, power becomes invisible while society remains trapped in visible conflicts. This strategy shields authority from criticism by dividing the public and weakening collective resistance.

Caste, for example, is used not merely as a social tradition but as a political resource. It divides society into permanent categories in which each group gradually comes to view its position as natural. When inequality is framed as something tied to birth, it moves beyond question. Structural injustice then appears as personal fate. Power no longer requires openly repressive policies; society itself sustains the existing order.

Religion provides identity with a moral vocabulary. It links the decisions of authority with morality, sanctity, and tradition. When policy is wrapped in religious sentiment, opposing it is portrayed not simply as political dissent but as moral transgression. Questioning becomes difficult because the questioner is quickly branded immoral, impure, or anti-social. In this process, reason recedes and emotion takes center stage.

The use of language as identity is subtle yet highly effective. Through language it is decided who belongs and who is an outsider. This classification does not remain cultural; it shapes access to resources, opportunities, and social respect. When superiority and inferiority are constructed on linguistic grounds, social unity fractures. Power benefits from this fragmentation because a divided society cannot articulate common demands.

The nation represents the broadest and most potent form of identity. It binds the individual to an imagined community, generating deep emotional attachment. Authority uses this attachment to place its decisions beyond scrutiny. When power presents itself as synonymous with the nation, criticism of power is redefined as hostility toward the nation itself. The distance between citizen and authority collapses, and the citizen begins to see the defense of power as a civic duty.

The greatest advantage of identity-based politics is that it overshadows real issues. Unemployment, inequality, lack of education, and health crises are complex and structural problems. Addressing them requires long-term policy, redistribution of resources, and confrontation with entrenched interests. By contrast, identity-based issues are simple, emotional, and capable of provoking immediate reaction. Power naturally promotes these simpler conflicts because they are safer.

When society remains trapped in internal conflicts, it ceases to question authority. Conflict redirects collective energy inward. People seek protection and solidarity within their own group rather than equal rights as citizens. Their identity as citizens recedes, replaced by identity as group members—and power capitalizes on this narrowing of perspective.

Division is often seen as a weakness of society, but for power it is its greatest strength. Because of division, authority no longer needs broad consensus; it only needs to ensure that no single group becomes strong enough to challenge it alone. When all groups compete against one another, power emerges as the mediator—and the mediator always controls the game.

A united society is dangerous for authority because unity generates questions. When people realize that their problems are shared and their origins common, the walls of identity begin to crumble. This moment is uncomfortable for power because emotional appeals cease to work; authority must then provide answers—and accountability runs contrary to its nature.

Therefore division is not merely tolerated; it is actively cultivated. In education, media, and public discourse, identity is placed at the center while structure is pushed into the background.

History is selectively presented so that present conflicts appear justified. Collective memory becomes a tool of politics.

Identity-based politics keeps society in a state of permanent insecurity. Every group is made to feel that its identity is under threat. In this atmosphere of constant danger, people willingly trade freedom for protection. Authority benefits from this exchange because a fearful society asks fewer questions and obeys more readily.

Throughout this process, power presents itself as a neutral observer, as though division were the natural condition of society. But division is not natural; it must be continuously reproduced. If this reproduction stops, society gradually begins to unite around shared interests. For that reason, identity must be repeatedly invoked, heightened, and framed as a site of conflict.

Welfare schemes appear humane and compassionate at first glance. They provide immediate relief—briefly quieting hunger, temporarily masking insecurity, and creating the impression that those in power understand social suffering. Yet there is a fundamental difference between relief and freedom. Relief postpones the crisis; freedom removes its roots. Power usually prefers the former, because the latter poses a risk to its very existence.

The objective of welfare is often not to eradicate poverty but to maintain it at a manageable level. Absolute poverty produces instability—hunger can spark rebellion. But controlled poverty is politically useful. When a person's basic needs are partially met, they are encouraged to feel grateful. That gratitude is converted into political capital—capital that can be traded for electoral support, social legitimacy, and claims of moral superiority.

Partial relief keeps people alive, but also keeps them dependent. Dependence becomes a form of security for power.

When the necessities of life flow from an external authority, people hesitate to confront it. Before asking questions, they worry that their fragile security might be withdrawn. Thus, welfare ceases to be merely an economic instrument; it becomes a tool for behavioral regulation.

Genuine empowerment—stable employment, quality education, and universal healthcare—creates real choices. Choices are threatening to power. A person with secure employment is not frightened by uncertainty. A person with education can distinguish between promises and outcomes. A person with healthcare protection makes decisions with confidence rather than fear. For this reason, these sectors are loudly announced but structurally weakened.

Welfare programs are usually tied to eligibility, conditions, and identity. It is determined who is "deserving" and who is not. This categorization is not merely administrative; it is political. Eligibility grants the power to select; selection grants the power to control. When assistance becomes charity rather than a right, it is placed beyond question. To question charity is framed as ingratitude.

In this arrangement, the individual ceases to be a citizen and becomes a beneficiary. A citizen demands rights; a beneficiary offers thanks. Power prefers beneficiaries, not citizens. Therefore, the language of welfare rarely becomes the language of rights. It remains the language of benevolence, help, and favour—a language in which power stands above and society remains below.

The instability of welfare schemes is not accidental. They are designed to improve life, but not to secure it. Insecurity keeps individuals alert, and this alertness is useful for maintaining control. When assistance becomes permanent and reliable, its political value declines. Intermittent relief repeatedly reminds people that their lives depend on the goodwill of authority.

Within this framework, poverty is treated not as a condition produced by structures, but as a problem of management. The question becomes not why poverty exists, but how it should be handled. Structural causes—unequal opportunity, concentration of resources, and the devaluation of labor—remain largely unaddressed because they are uncomfortable for power. Attention is directed toward symptoms, not causes.

Welfare also fragments social solidarity. When assistance is distributed through groups and categories, society loses the capacity to articulate common demands. Each group becomes invested in protecting its own share. In this competition, the underlying structure becomes invisible. Power benefits from this fragmentation because a divided society cannot demand systemic change.

The politics of gratitude is particularly effective. When assistance is presented as a gift, the fear of losing it accompanies acceptance. This fear produces silence. Individuals witness injustice, yet before speaking they recall that even their limited support can be taken away. In this way, welfare narrows freedom instead of expanding it.

Real empowerment is risky for power because it weakens intermediaries. Stable employment and education connect individuals directly to institutions, bypassing local patrons, brokers, and networks. The collapse of such dependency relationships creates instability for those who rely on them to rule.

Welfare, therefore, is often used not as a solution but as postponement. It buys time—political time, social time. Crises are deferred, not resolved. This postponement is presented as success. Statistics improve, while lived realities remain largely unchanged.

The distinction between welfare and empowerment is deliberately blurred. Relief is presented as development. Yet relief is not progress. Relief keeps people alive in the present; progress offers them a future. Controlling the present is easier for power; the future is uncertain.

The greatest illusion in this entire arrangement is that welfare proves the generosity of power. In reality, it is part of its survival strategy. Generosity is that which eliminates dependency; what strengthens dependency is not generosity—it is management.

The administrative apparatus appears formally impartial, rule-bound, and neutral. Constitutions, laws, manuals, and procedures create the impression that decisions are made by institutions, not individuals. In practice, however, administration is never truly separate from political power. Its neutrality largely exists on paper; in reality, it remains aligned with the interests of those who govern. This alignment is not the product of conspiracy, but of the incentives and sanctions within which administration operates.

Every administrative system disciplines itself through rewards and punishments. Those who comply with the expectations of power receive security, promotions, opportunities, and prestige. Those who ask questions, who prioritize the spirit of the law over its literal wording, become risks. They are labeled "difficult," "uncooperative," or "impractical." Obedience is institutionally rewarded, while dissent is relegated to the level of personal courage.

In countries like India, this process is especially subtle. The administrative structure emerges from a colonial legacy rooted in control and command. After independence the framework changed, but the psychological orientation did not entirely transform. Rules often serve not the citizen, but the stability of the existing order. Any official who challenges this stability—even in the name of public interest—is quickly viewed as "anti-system."

This pattern is not confined to India. In authoritarian regimes it is obvious: administration functions as an extension of power. In democracies it is more dangerous because it hides behind the mask of neutrality. Selective application of rules, the timing of investigations, and the movement of files become administrative weapons. Law exists, but its use follows the convenience of power.

The same logic operates globally. In many countries, bureaucracy is celebrated as a guardian of "stability." Stability, however, often means the preservation of the existing balance of power. Policies that threaten this balance—whether in the realm of the environment, labor rights, or social equality—are declared "unrealistic," "economically unsound," or "against national interest." Moral questions are thus reframed as technical difficulties.

The regime of rewards and punishments is not only formal but deeply informal. Transfers, confidential reports, departmental inquiries, and file delays all signal what behavior is acceptable and what is not. When officials witness careers stall for those who question, and flourish for those who remain silent, they learn the lesson. This learning is experiential rather than institutional—and therefore more powerful.

In such an environment, ethics stops being an institutional responsibility and becomes a private burden. Anyone who chooses an ethical course does so at personal risk. Institutions offer neither protection nor encouragement. Morality becomes an act of heroism—and heroism cannot be the foundation of any durable system. Systems require principles, but when principles inconvenience power, they are rarely institutionalized.

This tension is clearly visible in public services in India. Oaths of service, rules, and codes of conduct exist, but adherence is filtered through alignment with political authority. Officials who stay within the law yet make those in power uncomfortable find themselves isolated. Gradually, the message spreads: being "safe" matters more than being "right."

In much of the Global South the situation is even more intense because administration operates amid scarce resources and heavy political pressure. Yet the picture in advanced democracies is not entirely different. There, the administrative machinery is closely intertwined with corporate interests, financial institutions, and security establishments. Policies that challenge these interests are buried in technical complexities.

Another illusion of administrative neutrality is the claim that decisions are based on "data" and "expertise." What is rarely asked is who collects the data, whom the experts serve, and which questions are kept outside the scope of expertise. Expertise itself becomes an instrument of power. Moral disagreement is dismissed as ignorance or sentimentality.

Those who question the system do not simply act as individuals; they unsettle a structure that treats itself as natural. Therefore, the questioner must be marginalised. They are entangled in procedures, their intentions doubted, and eventually they are isolated. Meanwhile, those who remain silent, who follow "procedure" even when the procedure is unjust, are seen as "reliable."

Over time, the administrative machinery loses moral sensitivity. Decisions come to be based not on right and wrong but on safe and unsafe. This transformation is gradual; it is the product of years of institutional learning. A point arrives when witnessing injustice becomes routine, and challenging it becomes abnormal.

History contains many examples where administrative systems simply "followed orders," and later claimed that responsibility was not theirs. The justification remains the same everywhere: "We were only obeying the rules." But rules do not implement themselves; people do. When individuals detach themselves from moral responsibility, institutions become hollow.

In democracies this danger is deeper because public trust in institutions is at stake. When administration operates in alignment with power, public anger turns toward institutions themselves. The democratic framework weakens, even as political power manages to distance itself from blame. Institutions become shields.

The most dangerous outcome of this entire arrangement is that dissent gradually disappears—not only because it is suppressed, but because people grow tired and disillusioned. They learn that speaking out does not change outcomes, it only invites harm. This lesson becomes the most valued asset of power.

Corruption is commonly understood as a product of moral decline, lack of character, or individual greed. Public discourse often treats it as a problem of "bad people," as if removing a few individuals would purify the system itself. From the perspective of power, however, corruption is not an accident but a functional instrument. It plays the same role in the operation of power that grease plays in a machine—it does not make the machine ethical, but it certainly makes it run smoothly.

For power to remain stable, laws and legitimacy alone are insufficient; it also requires loyal networks. Every structure of power—democratic or authoritarian—depends on a select group of individuals through whom decisions are implemented. It is impossible to bind these actors solely through ideals. Here corruption enters. Illicit benefits generate shared interests, and shared interests generate shared silence.

When people participate together in illegal activity, an unwritten contract emerges among them. This contract is never documented, yet it is remarkably effective. Each participant knows that if even one person attempts to exit, the entire network may be endangered. Corruption therefore ceases to be mere monetary exchange; it becomes a politics of shared risk. This shared risk produces loyalty—not primarily through fear, but through mutual dependence.

In countries like India, where administrative systems are vast and complex, corruption often becomes the de facto means of "getting things done." Gradually, it shifts from being exceptional to becoming normal. A system that does not function according to rules begins to be operated from outside the rules. In this process, morality becomes irrelevant and pragmatism becomes the highest value. The honest are perceived as inefficient; those who compromise are labeled "practical."

This pattern is hardly confined to India. Across Latin America, Africa, Eastern Europe, and even developed democracies, corruption persists in varying forms—sometimes as bribery, sometimes as lobbying, sometimes as strategic exploitation of legal loopholes. The forms change, but the function remains constant: to sustain power-aligned networks.

A crucial aspect of corruption is that it reduces the distance between rulers and subordinates. When illegal gains are shared, formal hierarchies loosen and informal ties strengthen. These informal ties are more reliable for power because they are governed not by rules but by personal interests. Rules can be altered; interests endure.

Honesty, therefore, becomes destabilizing for such a system. The honest person is not merely a moral threat but a structural one.

They can disrupt the silence of the network, expose shared risks, and pull power into the realm of accountability. For this reason, honesty is often praised as a personal virtue but rarely encouraged institutionally. Corruption gives power another advantage: the capacity for selective punishment. When violations of rules become routine, the law cannot be applied uniformly. Power then acquires the discretion to decide when, against whom, and how enforcement will occur. Law becomes a tool of control rather than justice. Those close to power feel safe; those distant from it feel vulnerable. This selectivity is frequently visible in India. Large scandals may linger for years without decisive action, while minor infractions invite swift punishment. The message is unmistakable: the problem is not the crime, but the position of the criminal. An act becomes problematic only when committed outside power-aligned networks. The same logic operates globally. Financial crises, environmental disasters, and human rights violations have repeatedly occurred, yet responsibility rarely reaches those who made the decisive choices. Instead, blame is shifted downward onto lower-level officials or institutions. This production of "scapegoats" is another mechanism through which power protects itself. The most dangerous consequence of corruption is that it privatizes morality. Individuals are expected to remain ethical "within the system," even when the entire system is structured around unethical incentives. The result is a dilemma: either one compromises or one is marginalized. Most eventually choose the first path. Over time, society begins to normalize this condition. Outrage against corruption slowly turns into fatigue. People internalize the belief that "this is just how things are." This resignation is power's greatest victory, because it eliminates the need for open repression—society simply lowers its expectations. Corruption offers power short-term stability while simultaneously producing long-term decay. Institutions become hollow, trust erodes, and effectiveness declines. Yet power often prefers short-term security over long-term health. For power, it is better that the system rot slowly than face an abrupt challenge. It is also important to recognize that corruption is not limited to money. It appears in the form of positions, prestige, information, and protection. At times, it operates entirely within legal frameworks, yet remains morally corrosive. To understand corruption merely as "illegality" is therefore inadequate; it is the pragmatic face of the power structure itself. Foreign funds and external assistance are often presented as symbols of humanitarian concern, development, and stability. In public discourse, the belief is cultivated that outside resources will empower weak societies, strengthen institutions, and improve citizens' lives. Yet, once these resources enter the architecture of power, they assume a very different role. They frequently end up stabilizing and securing the very systems they claim to reform. The problem is rarely the volume of money; it lies in its direction and in the politics of dependence. When a government relies primarily on domestic taxation, an implicit social contract emerges. The taxpayer asks questions, and those in power are obliged to respond. This relationship may be imperfect and unequal, but a line of accountability remains visible. The moment state revenues begin to flow predominantly from external sources, that line grows faint. The survival of power then depends less on public consent and more on the continuity of external inflows. At this point, dependence replaces consent.

In countries like India, where the language of "aid" and "development" has been circulating for decades, foreign funding often becomes a tool of expansion rather than reform. The expansion, however, is not of social foundations but of security apparatuses, administrative reach, and surveillance systems. External resources are directed toward areas that deliver political value—control, stability, and visible achievements. Fields such as education, public health, and local self-governance, which have slow, uncomfortable, and transformative effects, are frequently pushed down the priority list.

On the global stage, this pattern becomes even clearer. In many countries, a substantial portion of foreign assistance is channeled into security cooperation, military training, surveillance technologies, and communication systems. The objective is not to improve citizens' everyday lives but to make regimes appear "reliable" and "stable." Stability here does not mean social justice; it means predictability—predictability that power will not suddenly collapse.

External funding confers another advantage on those in power: it allows them to distance themselves from domestic failures. When hospitals deteriorate or schools decay, authorities can invoke "resource constraints." Yet the same authorities may simultaneously spend lavishly on security infrastructure or propaganda campaigns. In such cases, the issue is not scarcity but priorities. Foreign assistance helps mask these priorities because it is presented as an "additional" stream of benevolent resources.

The politics of dependence reshapes not only the relationship between state and society but also social expectations. The language of rights slowly gives way to the language of aid. Instead of asking "What are we entitled to?", people begin to ask "What will we be given?". This shift is subtle but profound. Rights cultivate dignity; aid encourages gratitude. Gratitude is far more convenient for power.

In India and across much of the developing world, aid typically arrives in the form of projects—limited in time, scope, and ambition. A project concludes, a report is written, the funds cease, and the flow of documentation replaces the flow of change. Local capacity, institutional depth, and long-term structures lag behind. Assistance does not solve problems; it manages them repeatedly. Management is useful for power; resolution is risky.

There is also a conditional dimension to global assistance. These conditions are not always explicit, but they are effective. They influence policy choices, diplomatic positions, and economic directions. Governments present these constraints as "national interest" or "international obligations." Citizens neither fully know these conditions nor have the opportunity to deliberate on them. Power thus escapes dual accountability—neither completely answerable to its own people nor fully transparent to external donors.

A substantial portion of foreign funds also circulates within elite networks. Under the banners of consultancy, conferences, training, and representation, a class emerges that speaks the global language while remaining detached from local realities. This class is valuable to power because it mediates between external actors and domestic authorities. The social structure remains fragile, but representation shines.

Perhaps the most dangerous consequence of this process is that power adopts the language of reform while redirecting its orientation. Reform no longer means making institutions accountable to citizens; it means aligning them with external benchmarks. The standards change, but the distribution of power does not. Legitimacy is preserved; society remains weak.

Dependence fully displaces consent when citizens begin to believe that change no longer lies in their hands. Decisions seem to be taken elsewhere—far away, in inaccessible spaces. This perception breeds political disenchantment. Disenchanted citizens do not rebel; they adapt. Their resignation becomes another resource for power.

It is important to emphasize that external assistance is not inherently good or bad. Its effects depend on the structures into which it flows. When aid strengthens civic institutions, empowers local decision-making, and increases transparency, it can foster meaningful transformation. But when it is absorbed into mechanisms of control, it merely reinforces existing power.

India and numerous other countries demonstrate how efficiently power systems can absorb foreign capital. They translate it into their own language, priorities, and interests. As a result, the moral intent of aid and its political outcome often move in opposite directions. Power may change hands, but the logic of power does not. Any regime that comes to office follows the same fundamental rules: protect the ruling coalition, reward loyalty, and manage the rest of society. India is no exception in this regard. It does what power everywhere tends to do. The only difference is the idiom through which the process unfolds—elections, legal mechanisms, and nationalist rhetoric. The problem, therefore, does not lie in individuals but in the very structure of the system, where service to the people becomes a threat to power, and patronage becomes its moral duty.

CRITIQUE OF CAPITALISM

The term capitalism originates from the word capital, which refers not only to money but to all forms of accumulated wealth—land, property, machinery, technology, and other productive assets. In a capitalist framework, the underlying principle is straightforward: individuals may work according to their abilities, but the rewards they receive are largely determined by the amount of capital they already possess. Those who begin with greater capital typically secure higher profits and expand their wealth more rapidly.

At its core, capitalism is an economic system in which the majority of resources—land, industries, factories, and commercial enterprises—are privately owned. The role of the state remains comparatively limited, while private individuals and corporations drive economic activity. Although capitalism appears in multiple variants, several foundational features remain consistent:

1. Private ownership of property and production.
2. Minimal government intervention, expressed in the common maxim: *"The government has no business being in business."*
3. Market-driven competition, where businesses operate in an open marketplace.
4. Capital accumulation, where existing wealth generates further wealth through investment.

One of the most celebrated claims of capitalism is its supposed decentralisation. In theory, individuals are free to create their own enterprises, and thousands of new businesses emerge each year. These firms operate independently, competing with one another in ways that are believed to foster innovation and economic efficiency.

By contrast, in communist or socialist systems, the state typically exercises control over the major sectors of production. Industries and resources are directed through centralised planning, meaning that key economic decisions lie in the hands of a relatively small governing elite. This concentration of authority makes the management of an entire economy exceptionally complex and often prone to inefficiency.

One of the most frequently cited explanations for the United States' eventual dominance over the Soviet Union during the Cold War is precisely this difference in structure. The capitalist model in the United States was characterised by flexibility and decentralisation, allowing thousands of businesses to operate independently. Each enterprise competed with others, and this competition—driven by the pursuit of profit—encouraged continuous innovation. In contrast, the Soviet Union's rigid central planning frequently led to stagnation, resource misallocation, and the suppression of individual initiative.

Profit, indeed, has been the most potent incentive within capitalist systems. Firms strive to reduce costs, enhance efficiency, and introduce new products in order to survive and expand. Over the past two centuries, this profit-driven motivation has coincided with extraordinary technological advancements: automobiles, aviation, computing, the internet, smartphones, and more recently, artificial intelligence. Supporters of capitalism argue that no other economic system has generated such rapid progress in such a short historical span. They also highlight that, over the last fifty years, global poverty rates have declined, literacy has risen, and average living standards have improved significantly.

The narrative of capitalism is also built upon aspiration. It proclaims that anyone—regardless of background—can ascend to the top through talent, hard work, and perseverance. Biographical success stories of figures like Bill Gates, Elon Musk, and Jeff Bezos reinforce the belief that extraordinary wealth and influence are attainable for those who innovate and persist.

However, this narrative appears markedly different in the twenty-first century. The very companies once celebrated as symbols of entrepreneurial freedom—Amazon, Apple, Google, and Facebook—have grown so vast and influential that they operate almost like private governments. Instead of a marketplace filled with countless small competitors, we increasingly inhabit an environment dominated by monopolistic corporations that shape markets, control personal data, and influence public behaviour. While capitalism did catalyse significant innovation, it has also produced unprecedented levels of wealth concentration, reminiscent of the Gilded Age. Today, a small group of billionaires possess more wealth than several billion ordinary people combined.

Furthermore, the capitalist promise that "anyone can rise to the top" has proven largely illusory for most individuals. Structural inequalities—of class, caste, gender, ethnicity, and geography—continue to shape opportunity in decisive ways. For every entrepreneur who becomes a billionaire, millions labour under precarious and exploitative conditions: gig workers delivering food at low wages, warehouse employees monitored through surveillance systems, or factory workers in the Global South producing goods for consumers in richer nations. Even the widely-held claim that capitalism has reduced global poverty is heavily contested; while extreme poverty has declined, new forms of exploitation, debt dependency, and ecological devastation have expanded.

Consequently, the profit incentive that once drove technological progress now often fuels manipulation—whether through planned obsolescence in electronics, exploitative labour systems, or fossil-fuel industries that accumulate profit at the expense of planetary survival. Capitalism continues to innovate, but increasingly in ways that prioritise private accumulation over collective human well-being.

Capitalism often presents itself as the system of choices. In principle, a free market increases consumer options in every aspect of life. Take India as an example: for decades, state-run Doordarshan was the only television channel. Once the media sector was opened to private companies, dozens of channels flooded the market. Consumers suddenly had more choice, more variety, and arguably more entertainment value. Similar trends occurred in mobile networks, retail shopping, and even food delivery—capitalism diversified what was once uniform.

Supporters of capitalism point to this abundance of choices as evidence of its superiority. They argue that privatisation creates freedom, variety, and efficiency. But the story does not end here.

The same system that promises decentralisation and diversity often leads, paradoxically, to concentration and monopoly. While capitalism allows anyone to start a business, reality reveals a different pattern: smaller players are either crushed by competition or absorbed by larger corporations. Over time, what begins as a vibrant marketplace ends up dominated by a handful of giants.

This trend is not theoretical; it is our present reality. In India's e-commerce sector, Flipkart was once a homegrown success story—until Walmart bought it. In food delivery, Zomato and Swiggy have effectively carved up the market, leaving almost no space for newcomers. Globally, the situation is even starker: Google dominates search engines, Amazon controls online retail, Meta governs social networking, and Apple plus Microsoft shape the digital ecosystem.

The supposed freedom of consumer choice is now often an illusion. Yes, there are many channels on TV, but most are owned by a few conglomerates. Yes, there are countless apps in your phone, but they largely belong to the same set of tech giants. Behind the appearance of variety lies an unprecedented concentration of power.

The rise of monopolies has a direct connection with inequality. Once a company dominates a sector, it can dictate prices, suppress competition, and exploit workers. Profits accumulate in the hands of a few executives and shareholders while millions of workers face stagnant wages and insecure jobs. The world's richest 1% now own more wealth than the bottom half of humanity combined. In India, too, the pattern repeats: while billionaires like Mukesh Ambani or Gautam Adani expand their empires, ordinary citizens struggle with rising prices and precarious employment.

Thus, the *"freedom of choice"* celebrated by capitalism often masks a deeper reality: freedom for corporations to dominate, and inequality for everyone else. What begins as diversity ends as monopoly; what begins as opportunity ends as hierarchy.

When a company achieves monopoly power, the impact on consumers is severe. With no competitors to restrain it, the monopolist can raise prices, restrict services, or exploit its customers. In India today, many believe that Jio's dominance in the telecom sector has pushed competitors like Vodafone and Airtel to the brink, leaving consumers with fewer real choices and higher hidden costs. The promise of competition quickly fades once one giant controls the market.

Capitalism often operates under a brutal logic: either you swallow others, or you get swallowed yourself. Imagine a lake of fish—either a small fish devours others to grow, or a larger fish will devour it. This is precisely how corporate mergers and acquisitions unfold.

Take the case of Indian e-commerce and fashion retail. Jabong was absorbed by Myntra. Myntra itself was then absorbed by Flipkart. Eventually, Flipkart faced the same dilemma: surrender to Amazon or to another global giant. Walmart stepped in and acquired it. What looks like "growth" in capitalism is often nothing more than a chain of acquisitions until only a few titans remain.

The clearest examples of this cycle are visible in global technology. Facebook (now Meta) is a monopoly not just because of its platform, but because it swallowed Instagram and WhatsApp—two of the most widely used apps in the world. Google's dominance is even more comprehensive: YouTube, Android, Google Maps, Gmail, Google Drive, Google Pay, Google Cloud—all fall under its control. Few people realise that Google's parent company, Alphabet, has quietly acquired over 240 firms, ranging from AI startups to robotics to health-tech.

This pattern is not limited to Silicon Valley. In India, Reliance Industries is replicating a similar model: acquiring retail chains, digital platforms, and startups across diverse sectors, from groceries to streaming services. Adani Group too has expanded aggressively, taking over ports, airports, energy, and media. What emerges is not the picture of a free and competitive market, but of a handful of corporate empires that resemble private governments.

The outcome of this endless cycle of acquisitions is not greater freedom for the consumer or opportunity for the entrepreneur—it is growing inequality. Wealth becomes concentrated in fewer hands, while smaller firms disappear, workers lose bargaining power, and consumers find themselves trapped in ecosystems they cannot escape.

Thus, the *"Acquire or Be Acquired"* principle is not merely an economic strategy—it is the DNA of capitalism. And its natural product is monopoly, exploitation, and extreme inequality.

In theory, Capitalism promises competition, equal opportunity, and the freedom to succeed. In reality, however, the playing field is heavily skewed. Large corporations and wealthy individuals control vast portions of resources, markets, and infrastructure, making it almost impossible for small businesses to compete. For example, in India today, companies like Jio dominate telecom, while smaller providers struggle to maintain a customer base despite offering comparable services. Globally, tech giants like Amazon, Google, and Facebook have created monopolistic ecosystems that swallow smaller competitors or force them to merge.

Over the past 30–40 years, the resurgence of neoliberal policies has further accelerated this inequality. Wealth has become increasingly concentrated: as of 2017, the richest 1% of the global population captured more than 80% of new wealth created. Shockingly, just 42 individuals hold as much wealth as half the world's population combined. This is not evidence that billions of people are lazy while a few *"work harder."* The system is structured to favor those who already have capital. In other words, *"money begets money."* Those who start with wealth can invest, acquire, and expand with ease, while the poor are trapped in a cycle of scarcity. Without access to funds, the underprivileged struggle to invest in education, healthcare, or business, leaving them unable to accumulate wealth. according to Oxfam's 2025 report, the world's richest 1% have increased their wealth by over $33.9 trillion since 2015, which is more than enough to eliminate global poverty 22+ times over.

This structural imbalance has prompted some governments to step in with initiatives like free or subsidized education, microloans, and social welfare programs. Yet, these measures are often insufficient against the overwhelming power of global monopolies. The truth is that Capitalism, under its current form, does not reward hard work or innovation equally—it rewards existing wealth. Modern examples abound: startups in the shadow of corporate giants are either acquired at undervalued rates or forced out of the market entirely, illustrating the brutal reality of "acquire or get acquired." Meanwhile, ordinary workers often face stagnant wages, precarious employment, and rising costs of living, further reinforcing the cycle of poverty.

In essence, contemporary Capitalism magnifies inequality, concentrates power, and perpetuates systemic barriers that prevent genuine upward mobility. It is not merely a matter of effort or talent; the rules of the system themselves favor those already at the top.

Another major failure of Capitalism, and perhaps one of its most dangerous, is the destruction of the environment and society itself. Yes, in the past century, poverty rates have declined in many regions and literacy and education levels have risen—but the environmental damage we have caused in the same period is unlike anything the planet has seen in thousands of years. Deforestation is accelerating at unprecedented speeds, biodiversity is disappearing rapidly, and climate change is intensifying faster than ever before.

The reason is simple: under capitalism, companies prioritize profit above all else. Global consequences of deforestation, pollution, or ecosystem collapse are ignored as long as their balance sheets keep growing. This relentless pursuit of profit not only harms the planet but also has devastating social consequences.

While the system theoretically gives consumers choice, the reality is manipulated by corporate power. Modern advertising shapes desires and behaviors, often against people's well-being. Consider the global fast-food and sugary drink industries. Ads promote ultra-processed, high-fat, and chemically modified foods as sources of happiness and convenience. Social pressure—seeing friends, family, and peers consume these products—pushes individuals toward these unhealthy habits. Today, more than 34% of American adults are obese, and the U.S. ranks among the top countries for cancer rates linked to diet and lifestyle. These are capitalist societies where companies are free to market harmful products aggressively, all for profit.

The problem extends globally. In India, the rapid rise of processed food chains and sugar-laden beverages has caused obesity and diabetes to spike in urban areas. In Europe, meat and dairy industries continue large-scale deforestation in South America to feed growing demand. Meanwhile, tech giants and consumer goods corporations exploit natural resources without accountability, contributing to climate disasters—from floods in Pakistan to wildfires in Europe and North America.

Capitalism's obsession with profit, combined with global marketing and unchecked corporate power, ensures that short-term gains for a few come at long-term costs for everyone else. While markets celebrate "freedom of choice," this freedom is largely illusory when the system manipulates needs, desires, and consumption patterns, driving both societal health crises and environmental collapse.

In fact, in the race for profits, corporations have deliberately manipulated consumers into buying products that are harmful or unnecessary. Their strategy is simple: create demand for things people don't need and convince them that owning these products will give them social respect, status, or happiness. Classic examples include tobacco and alcohol industries, which advertise not just the product but the illusion of prestige, pride, or social acceptance that comes with consuming it.

But the impact of capitalism on consumer behavior extends far beyond these extremes. It has given rise to a culture of perpetual consumerism. Compare life today with life 50 years ago. Back then, a common person needed only a house, a stable job, and basic food to live a decent life. Now, to be considered "respectable" or "successful" in society, people are expected to own multiple gadgets, cars, smartphones, branded clothes, and constantly upgrade them. Owning the latest iPhone, the newest car model, or fashionable items every year is framed as essential for social acceptance.

This is not accidental. The system is designed to maximize continuous consumption, because the more people buy, the more profits companies generate. Advertising, influencer marketing, and AI-driven product recommendations have intensified this pressure in 2025.

The logic of capitalism treats resources as infinite and consumption as the ultimate metric of progress, while the reality is the exact opposite. Raw materials, clean water, rare minerals, and energy are all finite. Yet the system continuously pushes for more purchases, more upgrades, more "new" things—regardless of environmental or social costs. In the end, this profit-driven, infinite-consumption model benefits corporations, not society or the planet.

One of the most alarming consequences of capitalism is the large-scale environmental destruction we are witnessing today. But this destruction is not accidental—it is a direct outcome of a system designed to exploit human insecurities to drive consumption. Corporations constantly identify our fears, inadequacies, and desires, then sell products promising to "fix" them. If your skin is dark, buy a fairness cream. If you have unwanted hair, buy laser treatments. If your face, lips, or nose doesn't match a celebrity's, buy cosmetic surgeries. If you are short, buy growth drinks. This psychological manipulation fuels endless consumerism while depleting the planet's resources.

Beyond environmental and social harm, capitalism is increasingly failing to protect democracy. Historically, capitalism has been more compatible with democratic governance than communism, which often fell into dictatorship. Capitalism thrived alongside democratic structures for decades. But the system begins to fail when corporations grow so massive and wealthy that they wield power exceeding that of governments. Modern examples illustrate this clearly:

Political lobbying in the U.S.: Companies fund politicians and campaigns to ensure legislation favors their profits. This legally sanctioned influence often results in policies that prioritize corporate interests over citizens' welfare.

India and electoral bonds: It is almost impossible to track which corporations are funding which political parties. In practice, businesses support parties that maximize their benefits, often shaping policies, regulations, and land sales to their advantage.

Global environmental exploitation: Multinational corporations pressure governments to approve mining projects, deforestation, or industrial zones, even if these actions harm local communities and ecosystems. For instance, in 2025, deforestation in parts of the Amazon accelerated due to global agribusiness expansion, often with tacit or explicit government approval.

Tech monopolies and AI regulation: Major tech companies lobby governments worldwide to delay or weaken AI regulations, enabling unchecked surveillance, data harvesting, and influence over elections.

In these scenarios, governments often become puppets of corporate interests, prioritizing profits over people, democracy, and the environment. The logic is simple: the system rewards the accumulation of wealth, and wealth translates to political power. Meanwhile, citizens bear the costs—ecological destruction, social inequality, and manipulated democratic processes.

Capitalism, left unchecked, transforms democracy into a performance, consumerism into a societal mandate, and corporations into entities more powerful than the states themselves. The environmental, social, and political crises we face today are direct consequences of this profit-driven system.

Some historians see feudalism, around the 10th century, as an early precursor to capitalism. Landlords controlled vast territories, while peasants and laborers worked the land. Most of the harvest and profits went to the landlords, while the workers barely survived. The logic was simple: ownership and profit stayed with those who held property, not those who did the labor.

Even today, the logic remains the same. If you work at a company like Apple, your time, skills, and labor generate the product, but your salary is fixed. The actual profits go to shareholders—people who may not even know how an iPhone is made, but who earn huge returns simply because they own stock. In other words, money begets money: those with capital can multiply it, while workers remain dependent on wages.

Modern capitalism began to take shape in 16th–17th century Europe, particularly in Britain and the Netherlands. The Amsterdam Stock Exchange (1602) became the first stock exchange, and the Dutch East India Company pioneered issuing shares to raise capital. In the 18th century, Scottish economist Adam Smith, often called the father of capitalism, gave the system a clear theoretical framework. In The Wealth of Nations (1776), he argued for laissez-faire economics, where governments interfere minimally. He explained how competition—the "invisible hand"—drives innovation. If two pizza shops open in a neighborhood, they compete to make better and cheaper pizzas. Without regulation, the market itself pushes for efficiency.

Smith also highlighted division of labor, where different people handle specific tasks, improving speed and productivity. This principle fueled the Industrial Revolution, making mass production possible.

However, the system had a dark side. Early industrial workers faced exploitation, long hours, and unsafe conditions. Karl Marx highlighted this in Das Kapital, showing that specialization and efficiency came at the cost of human dignity: workers became alienated, performing repetitive tasks with no pride or purpose, reduced to replaceable cogs in the machine. Smith celebrated productivity; Marx warned it empowered capitalists to exploit labor. They observed the same system from opposite perspectives.

Capitalism does not always follow Smith's ideal of competition. In 1901, three major steel companies merged to form U.S. Steel, the first billion-dollar corporation. Instead of competing, they colluded to fix prices, creating a monopoly. Monopolies are like being stranded at night with only one taxi: the driver sets any fare, and you have no choice but to pay. Similarly, workers create products, but the surplus value—the extra profit—goes to owners and shareholders, not those doing the work.

The result is rising inequality. In the USA and other capitalist countries, wealth concentrates in fewer hands, while ordinary workers see minimal improvement in living standards.

Not all businesses must follow this exploitative model. Cooperatives offer an alternative. Take Amul, founded in 1946 under Tribhuvandas Patel, with guidance from Sardar Vallabhbhai Patel. Instead of distant investors, farmers collectively own Amul, and profits are returned to them. This demonstrates that capitalism can be reshaped if ownership is shared, providing a model where the laborers benefit alongside capital.

How does a simple paper note, a metal coin, or today even just a number on a mobile screen acquire the power to buy anything in the world? The very idea of money evokes images and emotions—coins, banknotes, digital balances, wealth, poverty, desire, power, and helplessness. But have we ever stopped to ask: what is money, really? How did it come into existence, and why does it dominate human life so completely?

Money is not eternal. Long ago, humans met their needs directly through barter. If I had extra wheat but wanted potatoes, and someone else had surplus potatoes but needed wheat, we could simply exchange. But this system had a critical limitation: the double coincidence of wants. Not only did you need to find someone who wanted what you had, but that person also needed to possess exactly what you needed. If I wanted shoes but the cobbler preferred vegetables, the trade failed. Barter was slow, inefficient, and limited.

As societies advanced, production increased, and human needs became more complex. Barter was no longer sufficient. People began to look for a universal medium of exchange, something everyone would accept for goods and services. Early forms of money varied—shells, grain, salt, and cattle—but each had flaws: perishability, difficult transport, and inconsistent quality.

Over time, societies turned to metals like gold and silver. These were durable, uniform, divisible, and highly concentrated in value, making them ideal for trade. Gold and silver became universal equivalents: now, if I had rice and wanted shoes, I could sell my rice for money and buy shoes from any cobbler, independent of his personal needs. Money transformed trade, allowing every commodity to express its value numerically: a shirt could be "₹100," a book "₹200." It became a measure of value, medium of circulation, store of value, and means of payment.

But money is not just a tool; it also carries a kind of fetishism. We treat it as if it holds magical power: with enough money, one can supposedly buy happiness, respect, or love. We forget that money is a social construct, a product of human labor and relationships. Gold and silver are valuable not inherently, but because society agreed to assign them that role. Change society's agreement, and money could be anything—a digital token, a resource, or even a cryptocurrency.

In capitalist society, however, this truth is obscured. Money is treated as an independent, controlling force, above humanity itself. Success is measured by accumulation, not by creativity, contribution, or relationships. We sacrifice community, well-being, and even morality in its pursuit. Money dominates our lives, from weddings and education to healthcare, social status, and friendships.

Cryptocurrencies like Bitcoin or Ethereum illustrate money as a social agreement: their value is not physical but agreed upon by millions globally. Yet they fuel speculation and wealth concentration in a few wallets.

Digital banking and mobile wallets make money instantaneous, creating a sense that wealth can grow endlessly through investments, stock trading, or apps like Robinhood and Zerodha. A student with ₹1,000 in an app can "own" shares worth millions on paper, reflecting capitalism's illusion of wealth multiplication.

Luxury and tech markets show money's fetishization: owning the latest Tesla, iPhone, or designer brand is seen as a symbol of identity, status, and success, even when basic needs remain unmet for billions.

Gig economy workers and freelancers often work long hours producing value for platforms like Uber, Amazon, or Fiverr, yet the digital money they earn represents only a fraction of the wealth they generate for the platform owners and investors.

Ultimately, real value lies not in coins, notes, or numbers on a screen, but in human labor, creativity, and relationships. Money is a claim on society's collective wealth. But under capitalism, it ceases to be a tool for meeting needs and becomes an end in itself—fueling endless accumulation, inequality, and the pursuit of wealth for wealth's sake.

One of the least discussed, yet most profound forms of violence within capitalism is the violence of time. This violence is neither visible nor criminalized in law; nevertheless, it functions as one of the greatest violations of human freedom in modern society. Capitalism does not merely exploit labor; it subordinates the very life-time of human beings. It extracts not only work, but the present, the future, and ultimately the very experience of living.

Time is the most finite resource available to human beings. Wealth can be accumulated, property can be acquired, and knowledge can be expanded—but lost time never returns. Yet within capitalism, time is treated not as an element of personal life but as a resource for economic production. A human lifespan is divided according to how much of it can be surrendered to the market.

In this system, time is not understood as value in itself, but as an input. Expressions such as "working hours," "productive time," and "working days" indicate that time has ceased to be a lived experience and has become an economic unit. An individual is not evaluated on the basis of what they think, feel, or mean to others, but according to how many hours they can work and how much output can be extracted from those hours.

This process intensified with the Industrial Revolution. Factories measured, regulated, and disciplined time. The clock ceased merely to mark life; it came to determine when one must work, pause, and return to work again. Gradually, this temporal discipline spread to offices, corporate institutions, and eventually to digital platforms.

Today, time is no longer confined to official working hours. Email, messaging applications, notifications, and expectations of constant online availability have dissolved the boundary between work and private life. The individual remains subordinated to work even outside the workplace. This is the permanent occupation of time.

Capitalist society divides life into two spheres:

1. Productive time (work)
2. Non-productive time (rest, relationships, reflection, thought)

The first is compulsory; the second, optional. Without the first, the second is impossible. Rest becomes not a right but a residual leftover after work. The central purpose of life shifts from "living" to "remaining employable."

The idealized balance—eight hours of work, eight of sleep, and eight of "the rest"—exists largely on paper. In reality, most people devote the best part of their day to work. Fatigue, commuting, psychological stress, and financial anxiety devour whatever so-called free time remains. Capitalism therefore creates the illusion that individuals control their lives while most of their time has already been predetermined.

Capitalism legitimizes this theft of time through necessity. People do not work primarily from free choice but in order to survive. Food, housing, healthcare, and education are subordinated to the market; therefore individuals must sell their time. Exploitation here is not overt but structural. No one may threaten them with weapons, yet the absence of viable alternatives functions as compulsion. Unemployment is reframed not as a structural outcome but as a personal moral failure.

In this way, capitalism transforms time from a sphere of free choice into the price of survival.

The greatest casualty of this theft of time is creativity and critical thought. Thinking, reading, questioning, and imagining all require time—and this is precisely what capitalism first removes. A person who spends most of the day exhausted, anxious, and pressured retains neither the energy nor the patience to question the system. A fatigued society becomes obedient without overt repression. Open coercion is less necessary when exhaustion does the work.

Knowledge itself is therefore converted into "skills." Education shifts from cultivating understanding to producing employability. A thinking individual may be dangerous; a skilled worker is not.

The temporal structure of capitalism has severe implications for mental health. The constant demand to remain productive fuses self-worth with work-worth. If one is not working, one is made to feel worthless. Hustle culture, burnout, anxiety, and depression are not merely individual conditions; they are symptoms of a system that treats human beings as machines—machines that are allowed to tire but not to feel.

In the digital age, the theft of time has become even more subtle. Not only working hours but human attention is commodified. Social media platforms no longer merely seek time; they seek continuous presence. Time is extracted not only as labor but as data and behavioral patterns. Individuals believe they are consuming entertainment, while it is in fact their time and attention that are being consumed and sold.

Capitalism thus produces a dual form of temporal control: the time of production and the time of consumption—both subordinated to the system.

This theft of time is not uniform. The wealthy can purchase time through paid services and care labor; the poor must sell their time. This is the most fundamental form of class division. Those who possess time can think, write, organize, and participate politically; those who lack it struggle merely to survive. Democracy itself becomes hollow when citizens lack the time necessary to engage meaningfully in it.

The most dangerous question for capitalism is not "Is this moral?" but "Is this necessary?" If people had sufficient time—to think, connect, and organize—they would question the supposed inevitability of the system. Genuine temporal liberation—less work, secure life, collective safety—directly challenges the logic of capitalism. This is why, despite technological advancement, working hours have not significantly declined; only surveillance has intensified.

Capitalism's deepest crime is not simply that it produces inequality, but that it quietly steals life itself—slowly, legally, and often with a smile.

The theft of time requires no prison, no handcuffs, no visible violence, yet its consequences are permanent: societies where people are alive, yet lack the time to live. Until time is liberated from the market, no economic reform can bring genuine emancipation. The first condition of freedom is not wealth but time.

In the modern era, the mental health crisis is typically framed as an issue of individual weakness, chemical imbalance, or poor life management. Stress, depression, anxiety, and burnout are interpreted as personal failures—as if the individual was not sufficiently positive, disciplined, or hardworking. This interpretation is not only incomplete but also dangerous, because it renders the structural causes of psychological suffering invisible.

In reality, the contemporary mental health crisis is not the outcome of personal defects, but the inevitable result of a socio-economic order that defines human beings primarily as units of production and agents of consumption. Capitalism has normalized psychological distress; it is no longer an exception but the prevailing condition.

Capitalism subjects mental health to the logic of the market. Identifying anxiety, depression, and exhaustion as "illnesses" is not the problem in itself; the problem begins when their causes are severed from social structures and located exclusively within the individual. Solutions are sought in medication, motivational rhetoric, and mindfulness applications, while the conditions that generate stress remain unchanged. In this way, capitalism converts psychological suffering into a private problem, ensuring that the system itself escapes scrutiny.

This process produces a double benefit: (1) the system avoids criticism, and (2) mental health becomes a profitable industry.

In capitalist society, self-worth is tied to productivity. The question “What do you do?” gradually becomes synonymous with “Who are you?” If one is employed, one is useful; if not, one is a failure. This permanently destabilizes self-image. Individuals live in a constant state of self-justification—before employers, society, and eventually before themselves. Rest, slowness, and stillness are reinterpreted as laziness or weakness. In such an environment, mental peace is not a natural condition but a rare achievement.

Hustle culture is not merely a culture of working more; it is a moral framework. Fatigue is glorified, and rest is viewed with suspicion. Within this morality:

1. sleeping less becomes a badge of honor
2. constant busyness is read as success
3. exhaustion is seen as personal inadequacy

This moral pressure compels individuals to work against the signals of their own bodies and minds. Burnout therefore is not an accident; it is a systemic outcome.

Capitalism is grounded not in stability but in competition and uncertainty. Job security, health security, and guarantees about the future are diminishing. The gig economy, contract work, and freelancing are framed as “freedom,” while in reality they produce permanent precarity. This insecurity is not merely economic; it is psychological. Individuals are constantly anxious about the next month, the next project, the next opportunity. Continuous uncertainty consumes mental energy and prevents people from living in the present.

Capitalism thrives on comparison. Social media, advertising, and consumer culture constantly remind individuals that someone else is earning more, looking better, achieving faster, and living a superior life. These comparisons are not organic; they are designed. Algorithms detect insecurities and deepen them. The result is self-doubt, envy, and inferiority. Mental health erodes under this relentless evaluative gaze.

Corporate culture treats emotions as obstructions. Sadness, fear, confusion, or insecurity are labeled "unprofessional." Individuals are expected to conceal their struggles and perform constant competence and positivity. This emotional labor weighs heavily on mental health: people do not merely work—they continually perform. The dual burden of labor and masking intensifies psychological exhaustion.

The digital era has further complicated the crisis. Individuals are exhausted not only by work but also by the overwhelming flow of information. Notifications, emails, messages, and updates fragment attention. This perpetual attentional disruption weakens concentration; people lose the capacity for deep thought or sustained feeling. This manifests as digital burnout.

The mental health crisis does not affect everyone equally. Those with economic security can purchase therapy, treatment, and rest; those without resources lack both time and access. The poor are expected to continue working despite psychological suffering. Mental health thus becomes a class privilege.

The dominant capitalist perspective treats mental health as an issue of individual treatment rather than social transformation. Medication and therapy can address symptoms, but they cannot alter the system that continuously produces psychological distress. This is akin to handing out masks in a toxic environment while refusing to remove the poison.

The contemporary mental health crisis is not a mysterious epidemic. It is the predictable consequence of a system that demands ever more from human beings while denying them security, time, and dignity.

Education is commonly regarded as the foundation of human progress, a vehicle for social transformation, and a source of intellectual freedom. Historically, its purpose was to enable human beings to think, question, understand, and act as responsible participants in public life. However, within the modern capitalist order, education has gradually drifted away from this original purpose and has been converted into a market commodity. It is no longer primarily the expansion of knowledge; it has become an investment, a certificate-producing industry, and a pathway to employment.

Capitalism has redefined education not as a public and human right but as a form of private economic property. This redefinition has profoundly shaped the structure, content, objectives, and ethics of education. In capitalist logic, the value of education is determined by its "utility" in the market. This utility does not mean understanding or wisdom; it means skills—skills tailored to the needs of industries, corporations, and the corporate economy. The aim of education shifts from developing comprehension to enhancing employability.

As a result, education is transformed from a broad cultivation of thought into a narrow training mechanism. Students do not primarily learn how society functions; they learn how to "fit" into it. Education is not seen as a lived experience but as an investment in future income. Students and families increasingly approach education with a single question: How much salary will this bring? The value of learning is thus measured not in intellectual or ethical terms but in financial returns. Choices of discipline reflect market value rather than curiosity or passion. Failure is not perceived as an intellectual exploration but as a loss on investment. Learning becomes saturated with anxiety and competition. The student ceases to be a curious mind and becomes a risk manager.

Privatization of education in capitalism rests on the belief that markets improve quality. In practice, privatization does not make education better—it makes it more unequal. Private institutions charge high fees, package education as a brand, and link access less to merit than to the ability to pay. Consequently, quality education becomes concentrated in the hands of a privileged class. For the poor and the marginalized, education turns from an opportunity into a struggle. A system that could have reduced inequality begins instead to reproduce it.

Examinations in the capitalist education system cease to be instruments of learning and become filters. To pass these filters, a vast coaching industry emerges—built on fear, intense competition, and an extremely narrow definition of success. Failure is individualized and moralized. Coaching culture reduces education to ranks and scores; students memorize patterns rather than develop understanding. The capacity to adapt replaces the capacity to think.

When education is presented as the only ladder to success, academic failure becomes existential. Students begin to internalize the belief that failure in exams or careers is failure in life itself. This psychological burden produces anxiety, depression, and in extreme cases, suicide. Learning becomes inseparable from fear. This is not an individual weakness but the direct outcome of a system that binds the worth of life to economic achievement.

Capitalist education is uncomfortable with critical thinking. A questioning student is not a productive employee but a potential critic of the system itself. Hence curricula are sanitized and depoliticized; contentious social, political, and economic questions are avoided. The ideal student is obedient, adaptable, and "market-ready." The system does not cultivate its critics; it manufactures conformity.

As access to education expands, the value of degrees simultaneously declines. Bachelor's degrees become ordinary, then master's degrees follow, and specialized certificates proliferate. This "credential inflation" traps individuals in an endless academic race, consuming time and resources while inflating paper qualifications rather than knowledge. It does not solve the employment crisis; it conceals it.

Ultimately, capitalist education reshapes itself according to the needs of the labor market. Universities design curricula for industries rather than for society. Education becomes market-dependent rather than autonomous. It does not ask what society requires for justice, democracy, or human flourishing; it asks what industry demands for profit.

Health is generally regarded as a fundamental human right—a condition that allows individuals to live physically, mentally, and socially balanced lives. Yet within a capitalist system, health gradually ceases to exist as a human condition and is instead transformed into an economic sector. In this framework, health no longer signifies well-being or wholeness; it comes to represent the continuous expansion of treatment, pharmaceuticals, insurance, and healthcare services.

Capitalism is not primarily concerned with improving health, but with managing illness and converting it into profit. The distinction is subtle but decisive. The purpose of health is human well-being, while the purpose of the market is profit maximization. This contradiction lies at the core of the modern healthcare crisis.

Within capitalist logic, health is defined negatively—not as a positive state of well-being, but merely as the absence of disease. The consequences are predictable. Prevention, lifestyle, social determinants, and environmental causes are marginalized, while treatment becomes central. Illness is no longer a failure of the system; it becomes an opportunity: More disease leads to more patients, more patients lead to more treatment, more treatment leads to more profit. A system emerges in which complete health becomes economically undesirable.

Modern healthcare has evolved into an extensive network of hospitals, pharmaceutical corporations, diagnostic laboratories, medical device manufacturers, and insurance companies. Their shared objective is not to keep people healthy, but to extract revenue from health itself.

Within this system, treatment becomes a commodity, the patient becomes a customer, and the doctor becomes part of a managerial and corporate structure rather than an independent healer. Health decisions increasingly shift from ethical or scientific reasoning toward economic calculation.

Privatization claims that competition improves quality. In reality, it deepens inequality rather than enhancing care. In privatized healthcare systems, quality treatment becomes linked to the ability to pay, healthcare becomes a luxury for the poor, and the difference between life and death is increasingly determined by bank balance. Health—an area that should reduce inequality—ends up reinforcing class divisions.

Health insurance is presented as protection, yet under capitalism the insurance sector does not share risk; it filters it. Insurance companies evaluate profitability before illness, entangle treatment in conditions and exclusions, and convert human suffering into paperwork, delays, and procedural obstacles. The individual feels secure, but in reality is only managing uncertainty.

The pharmaceutical industry represents one of the most powerful arms of modern capitalism. Its research priorities rarely aim at eradicating disease entirely. Instead, emphasis is placed on drugs that must be consumed continuously over long periods of time. As a result, lifestyle diseases become permanent markets, symptoms are treated while causes are ignored, patients become lifelong consumers, and cure is replaced by dependence.

The most effective and affordable form of healthcare is prevention: clean environments, nutritious food, safe working conditions, and psychological well-being. Yet these measures generate little profit. Within capitalist logic, a healthy society does not consume enough, while an unhealthy society becomes a continuous market. Preventive policies are therefore neglected, while expensive treatments are promoted and celebrated.

Capitalist healthcare also places doctors in a moral dilemma. Although they swear to serve the patient, they operate within institutions where revenue targets exist, bed-occupancy rates are monitored, and tests and procedures are tied to income streams. The doctor–patient relationship shifts from humane care toward transactional interaction.

Within this framework, the value of health lies not in human life itself, but in labor capacity. People are maintained in health only as long as they remain productive. Once they are deemed "unusable"—the elderly, the disabled, or the terminally ill—they are treated as burdens on the system. Human dignity recedes, and life is measured in terms of productivity.

Pandemics expose the contradictions of capitalist healthcare with brutal clarity. Crises reveal that privatization cannot guarantee collective security, markets cannot make ethical decisions under emergency conditions, and health is a public necessity rather than a private commodity. Yet once the crisis subsides, the system returns to its earlier patterns.

When health becomes a market, illness is moralized. Patients are encouraged to blame themselves—for lifestyle choices, discipline, or personal failure—while the social and structural causes of disease remain invisible. Suffering becomes individualized, and solidarity dissolves.

Under capitalism, healthcare has transformed into a health-management industry. Its interest lies not in reducing illness, but in controlling and monetizing it. Until health is liberated from the logic of profit, medicine will continue to function as commerce rather than human service. Where life is subordinated to profit, health can never become truly universal.

Human dignity means that the value of a person arises simply from their existence—not from their utility, productivity, or economic capacity. Dignity affirms that every individual deserves respect regardless of how much they earn, how much they work, or how useful they are to the market. Capitalism, however, stands in sharp contrast to this principle.

Capitalism does not recognize human beings for simply being human; it recognizes them through production and consumption. In such a system, dignity ceases to be an inherent quality and becomes a conditional status—granted only so long as an individual remains useful to the market.

Capitalist logic reduces the human being from a social and moral subject to an economic unit. The language itself exposes this transformation: worker, consumer, customer, human resource. The individual is no longer seen as a person, but as a function.

Within this framework, the body becomes a machine for labor, the mind a center for skill production, and time a commodity for sale. Once a person is viewed as a resource, dignity inevitably becomes secondary.

The most dangerous illusion promoted by capitalism is the belief that a person's worth is determined by their productivity. Those who produce more are considered more valuable. The consequences are immediate and severe: the unemployed are labeled "useless," the elderly are treated as burdens, and persons with disabilities are reduced to objects of sympathy rather than recognized as equal holders of rights. Dignity becomes conditional.

In capitalist culture, poverty is not treated merely as an economic condition but is moralized. The poor are portrayed as lazy, incapable, or undeserving. In this way, the system absolves itself of responsibility and transforms structural inequality into individual failure. This moralization erodes social empathy, conceals structural exploitation, and replaces dignity with shame.

In modern society, identity has become deeply welded to work. "What do you do?" has become the primary question of social interaction. Gradually, work eclipses the person. In such a world, the unemployed become invisible, rest and idleness begin to feel like crimes, and life beyond employment becomes difficult even to imagine. Dignity collapses into a single dimension: economic function.

Capitalism also ties dignity to consumption. Better clothes, larger houses, and expensive education become markers of respect. Dignity shifts from inner worth to outward display. Those who cannot consume are denied recognition and respect.

The system renders invisible all forms of labor that do not generate profit—domestic work, caregiving, emotional labor. These forms of work sustain society, yet hold little or no value in the market. Their devaluation disproportionately undermines women's dignity and normalizes exploitation by disguising care as "natural duty."

Under capitalism, human rights are often subordinated to market rights. Property, profit, and contractual freedom are placed above life, health, and respect. As a result, life becomes subordinate to profit, justice becomes tied to the ability to pay, and dignity becomes economic rather than legal or moral.

Where inequality exists, dignity cannot remain equal. Capitalism concentrates wealth and power in a few hands, allowing those who control resources to define what counts as "respectable." Workers are expected to remain grateful, assistance is framed as charity rather than right, and dissent is labeled ingratitude.

When people are repeatedly told that their value depends on output, their existence becomes insecure. Self-respect becomes dependent on external approval, existential anxiety increases, and life turns into a continuous process of self-evaluation. Yet dignity is not something to be earned; it is innate.

Modern capitalism presents itself as neutral, global, and opportunity-creating. It claims that free markets and globalization offer equal chances to everyone. This narrative conceals reality. The world is not structured into equal units, but into profoundly unequal zones of power, resources, and labor.

On one side lies the so-called Global North, where capital, technology, and decision-making are concentrated. On the other lies the Global South, which supplies cheap labor, raw materials, and environmental sacrifice. This division is not accidental; it is a structural requirement of capitalism.

The wealth of industrial powers rests on colonial exploitation. Although colonial rule has formally ended, its economic architecture persists. Multinational corporations, financial institutions, and trade regimes function as instruments of neo-colonial control.

Capitalism seeks maximum profit at minimum cost. The Global South fulfills this logic through low wages, weak labor rights, fragile unions, and lax environmental regulations. Production occurs in the South, while profits accumulate in the North. Sweatshops represent capitalism in its most exposed form—long hours, unsafe conditions, and minimal wages—while finished products are sold cheaply to consumers who rarely confront the human cost paid in health, life, and dignity.

Natural resource extraction follows the same pattern. Minerals, oil, timber, land, and water are extracted for global markets, leaving behind ecological destruction, displacement of indigenous communities, and long-term environmental crises. The benefits flow outward; the damage remains local.

International debt further deepens subjugation. Loans are tied to conditions such as privatization, welfare cuts, and reduced public spending. Sovereignty is weakened, and policy decisions are placed under external control—economic domination without visible empire.

The migration of skilled workers—doctors, engineers, scientists—drains the Global South of talent developed through public investment. Local systems weaken while already powerful economies grow stronger.

Global crises intensify these inequalities. Those least responsible for climate change suffer its worst consequences. Those most affected by economic recessions possess the fewest tools for recovery.

Capitalism no longer exploits only labor and resources; it now penetrates human consciousness. Industrial capitalism exploited labor, consumer capitalism exploited desire, and surveillance capitalism exploits behavior itself.

Its primary resource is data—extracted silently from daily life. Every click, search, pause, and movement becomes raw material. Data is not merely information; it is a map of behavior. The objective is no longer prediction alone, but control.

Surveillance is normalized through convenience and security. Privacy is framed as obsolete, and "having nothing to hide" is treated as virtue. Attention is harvested as algorithms privilege outrage, fear, and stimulation over reflection and depth. Freedom is simulated through choice, while the choices themselves are engineered.

Privacy is not only a personal right; it is a precondition for free thought. Constant observation produces self-censorship, suppresses dissent, and leaves democratic forms intact but hollow.

In surveillance capitalism, the user is not the customer; the user is the product. Data is extracted without fair compensation, consent remains ambiguous, and power concentrates in a few corporations. Resistance is difficult precisely because the system is invisible, convenient, and embedded in daily life. Where profit defines value, human dignity is always at risk.

Capitalism presents itself as an efficient system of resource allocation. It claims that markets balance demand and supply to ensure optimal use of resources. In reality, capitalism depends on scarcity—and much of this scarcity is artificially produced.

Without scarcity there is no value; without value there is no profit. Capitalism therefore requires the continued existence of deprivation—whether of food, housing, healthcare, education, time, or security. The result is a world where abundance coexists with hunger, homelessness, and precarity.

Natural scarcity arises from genuine physical limits. Artificial scarcity is created through social and economic institutions. Today, enough food is produced, the capacity to build adequate housing exists, and technology and knowledge are widely available. Yet millions remain excluded. This contradiction is structural, not natural.

In capitalist agriculture, food is produced for profit, not for nourishment. Grain is destroyed to prevent price collapse, farmers suffer losses amid surplus, and hunger is reframed as a lack of purchasing power rather than systemic failure.

In cities, millions remain homeless while millions of houses stand empty. This is not a housing crisis but a crisis of ownership and speculation. Homes become investment instruments, appreciating assets, and stores of profit rather than places to live.

Medicines and treatments are kept artificially expensive through patents and monopolies. Life-saving treatments exist but remain inaccessible. Disease becomes profitable, and health becomes transactional rather than a right.

Education, despite being digitally shareable at negligible cost, is kept scarce through degrees, certifications, and selective access. This is not a scarcity of talent, but of opportunity.

Unemployment persists not because work is absent, but because employment is organized to maintain competition, suppress wages, and discipline labor. Artificial unemployment is essential to capitalism.

Scarcity is also a political tool. When people believe resources are limited, they compete, view others as threats, and stop questioning the system. Social solidarity fractures, and control becomes easier.

Capitalism displays abundance through endless commodities, but real security—health, housing, time, dignity—remains scarce. Needs are commodified, commodities are artificially restricted, and scarcity becomes profitable.

Capitalism claims to offer equal opportunity, attributing outcomes to talent and effort. This rhetoric conceals its core logic. Inequality is not an accident of capitalism; it is its structural necessity.

Profit requires cheap labor, concentrated resources, and economic insecurity. If people possessed genuine security and freedom, exploitative conditions would be refused. Capitalism therefore requires inequality to survive.

Labor markets function only when workers outnumber jobs. Unemployment is not a failure of capitalism but a condition of its success. Wealth becomes power, shaping policy, markets, and ideology. Accumulation is rewarded; redistribution is resisted.

Opportunities are inherited, not distributed equally. Some begin far ahead; others never reach the starting line. Yet outcomes are moralized as merit.

Consumer culture depends on inequality. Status requires comparison, scarcity, and perpetual upgrading. Economic power translates into political power, hollowing democracy.

Technology reorganizes inequality rather than abolishing it. If everyone had security, free time, and the option not to work, capitalist discipline would collapse. Inequality is not capitalism's outcome—it is its method.

Capitalism is not dehumanizing because it is openly cruel, but because it is indifferent. It recognizes profit, not pain; growth, not lives. Any system that does not place human beings—along with time, dignity, relationships, and the environment—at its center may appear advanced, but ultimately stands opposed to humanity.The crisis of capitalism is not merely economic. It is existential.

CONSUMERISM

Consumerism is often seen as a superficial phenomenon—merely synonymous with "buying more" or a "luxury lifestyle." But this understanding deeply underestimates its true nature. Consumerism is not an individual habit or personal weakness; it is a systemic ideology that developed organically alongside modern capitalism and gradually restructures how humans think, feel, and live. If capitalism is the economic framework of production and profit, consumerism is its cultural and psychological extension. It does more than expand markets; it positions humans in a role where their primary identity is defined not as citizens, workers, or social beings, but as consumers.

Consumerism is a form of desire-based control. It does not force individuals to act; rather, it conditions them to want exactly what the system wants. In this process, obedience merges with pleasure, making consumerism all the more insidious. When individuals begin to perceive their desires as freedom, they fail to recognize where those desires originate. This illusion of freedom is consumerism's most powerful weapon.

Consumerism influences not just economic behavior, but also culture, morality, identity, and social relations. Concepts like success, happiness, self-respect, and even love and care have been translated into market language. We no longer ask, "Who am I?" but rather, "What can I afford?" Human worth is no longer intrinsic; it is measured by purchasing power and consumption capacity. This transformation affects not only individuals but society as a whole, creating a psychologically fragile community perpetually trapped in comparison, competition, and dissatisfaction.

The rise of consumerism is no coincidence. As capitalism generated mass production and surplus, a structural challenge emerged: who would buy all this output? The solution was less economic and more psychological. Humans needed to be transformed into permanent desire-machines, not just buyers. Advertising, branding, media, and later digital platforms created a culture where satisfaction became temporary and craving permanent. Understanding consumerism is, in essence, understanding capitalism's survival strategy.

Modern systems of domination often operate invisibly. While religion controlled through belief and nationalism through identity, consumerism enforces obedience through pleasure and comfort. People interpret their exhaustion, anxiety, and emptiness as personal failure rather than systemic outcomes. They work more and consume more, hoping that the next product, upgrade, or lifestyle will bring fulfillment. Consumerism creates a self-reinforcing loop in which even suffering becomes a market opportunity.

Exploitation is often thought of in terms of factories, labor, or wages, but consumerism shifts it to the level of the mind. Here, exploitation means not just extraction of surplus value, but extraction of attention, time, desire, and identity. Even mental space becomes a battlefield for the market.

To understand consumerism, it is crucial to recognize that it is not a timeless human tendency. Humans have always used things, but purchasing them and building identity through objects is a relatively modern phenomenon. Pre-capitalist societies had largely need-oriented economic activity. Production was limited, technology constrained, and resources operated under scarcity.

Consumption focused on survival, stability, and social continuity. Clothing, tools, food, and shelter were functional, with minimal symbolic or identity-based meaning. Social status depended more on birth, community, or role than on possessions.

The Industrial Revolution decisively disrupted this balance. Mechanized production and factory systems enabled mass production, generating unprecedented market surpluses. Capitalism faced a new structural challenge: how to ensure demand as production capacity rapidly increased. Consumption gradually shifted from need to desire. Products were marketed not only for utility but for differentiation. Packaging, branding, and early advertising began to make identical products appear distinct to sell more.

The twentieth century marked a decisive turning point for consumerism. Advertising became a scientific industry rather than casual commercial practice. Psychology, behavioral studies, and later psychoanalysis were used to understand that humans are not just rational buyers but emotional, insecure, and socially influenced beings. After the World Wars, especially in Western economies, consumerism was promoted deliberately as a tool for economic stability and social control. Mass consumption was framed as patriotism, progress, and a symbol of modern life. Consumers were no longer mere buyers but engines of economic growth.

Post-war capitalism converted consumerism into a cultural ideology. Television, cinema, and later print media created an aspirational culture linking happiness, success, and respect with products. Consumption acquired symbolic meaning. Clothing, cars, gadgets, and lifestyle choices became markers of social identity. People no longer asked, “Is this useful?” but rather, “What does this say about me?" Consumerism crystallized as an identity-forming mechanism.

In the late twentieth and early twenty-first centuries, consumerism became even more sophisticated. Globalization and digital technology made markets borderless, and advertising hyper-personalized. Data analytics, algorithms, and social media predicted and shaped consumer desires with unprecedented precision. Consumerism moved from mass culture to individual-level psychological operation, generating tailored desires, curated lifestyles, and algorithm-driven aspirations. It became a continuous background process, functioning not only during shopping moments but throughout daily scrolling, watching, and interacting.

At every stage, consumerism was presented as natural and inevitable. Each technological and cultural shift was framed as progress, while in reality, these shifts served capitalism's structural needs. The expansion of consumerism was not a sign of human freedom but a mechanism for system survival. As production and markets expanded, human desires were similarly expanded and re-engineered. Consumption was normalized as a moral duty: buying was necessary for economic growth, adopting new products was proof of modernity.

The defining feature of consumerism is not that people buy things, but that they learn to desire things they never truly needed. This "wanting" is not a natural or spontaneous process; it is a systematically engineered outcome. Modern capitalism has developed an infrastructure where desires are created, stimulated, and sustained with scientific precision. Advertising, branding, media, psychology, and digital technology work together to keep the consumer in a constant state of dissatisfaction and aspiration.

Need is a finite endpoint, but desire is deliberately made endless—because a satisfied consumer is useless for the system.

The first step in this manufacturing is the creation of insecurity. Consumerism does not explicitly say "you are incomplete," but subtly generates this feeling through imagery, narratives, and social comparisons. Body image, lifestyle, career success, relationships, and even happiness are projected as idealized standards. Any deviation from this ideal is framed as deficiency. Humans naturally compare themselves, and when they perceive a gap, the market offers ready-made solutions—products, services, or lifestyle choices. This creates a problem–solution loop in which the problem is artificial, and the solution commodified.

The second layer converts emotions into commodities. Products are no longer merely functional; they carry emotional promises—confidence, attraction, respect, belonging, control. These promises bypass rational evaluation. Behavioral psychology shows that human decision-making is largely emotional and subconscious. Advertising exploits this vulnerability. Through repetition, music, color, celebrity endorsements, and storytelling, a product becomes associated with an emotion, making the consumer believe they are buying the feeling, not the item.

The third mechanism is habit and addiction formation. Modern consumerism does not simply create desire; it makes that desire repeatable and compulsive. Dopamine-based reward cycles, scarcity cues, limited editions, and constant novelty put consumers into a loop where anticipation is more rewarding than actual consumption. Once one desire is satisfied, the system immediately presents the next one. Satisfaction is intentionally short-lived so that craving remains permanent. Consumerism thus becomes a psychological treadmill—movement is mandatory, stopping is not allowed.

The digital age has taken this manufacturing to unprecedented levels. Algorithms and data analytics track consumer behavior, preferences, and vulnerabilities. Desire is no longer mass-level but customized to the individual. Social media platforms are no longer mere communication tools; they are desire-distribution systems. Influencers, curated lifestyles, and algorithmic recommendations colonize consumer imagination. People perceive their desires as personal, but they are the product of data-driven predictions.

Another important aspect of this manufacturing is that consumerism consumes time and attention. Desire is not only for products but also for anticipation, research, comparison, and display. The consumer's cognitive space is continuously occupied by the market, leaving little room for reflective thinking. People interpret their dissatisfaction as personal failure rather than systemic manipulation.

The most disturbing implication of this manufacturing is that it leaves people perpetually incomplete. The self never feels "enough"; it is always chasing the next purchase, the next upgrade, the next identity. Autonomy and agency gradually erode. Individuals stop examining their desires and simply follow them. Consumerism becomes a form of discipline in which obedience is given not to an external authority but to one's own cravings.

Consumerism presents itself in the language of freedom. Markets claim that the consumer is independent, autonomous, and empowered—they can buy what they want, choose any brand, and design their life as they please. On the surface, this seems convincing: shelves are full, online platforms show infinite options, and every product claims to be "different" and "unique." Yet, a critical examination reveals that most of this freedom is an engineered illusion.

The first layer of this illusion is pre-structured options. Consumers choose only among the options the market has pre-selected. They do not decide what will be produced, how it will be produced, or under what logic the options are made available. Corporate power, profit calculations, and market research have already fixed these decisions. The consumer's role is limited to selecting an item from a curated menu—like choosing a dish at a restaurant. Consumers rarely question this reality, because the experience of choice feels like freedom.

The second layer is the myth of brand differentiation. Every product is presented with a distinct identity—premium, budget, ethical, cool, minimalist, rebellious, traditional. Consumers perceive these categories as reflecting their personality and values. Deeper analysis shows that most brands serve the same structural system. Differences lie in packaging, narrative, and marketing, not in purpose or impact. Consumers feel their choice is expressive, but they are exercising only aesthetic preference within the system's framework. Freedom exists in presentation, not in substance.

The third layer is psychological conditioning. The illusion of choice is reinforced when consumers perceive their decisions as entirely personal. Preferences do not arise in a vacuum—they are shaped continuously by culture, media, peers, social norms, and algorithms. Consumers perceive their taste as "natural," though it is the result of long-term conditioning. When something becomes repeatedly visible, socially rewarded, and aspirational, it ceases to be a choice and becomes the default. Consumers feel they are choosing freely, but their options are pre-selected mentally.

Digital capitalism has strengthened this illusion. Algorithms observe behavior and present personalized options. This personalization feels like freedom but increases predictability.

Consumers are shown what they are already conditioned to expect, limiting experimentation and deviation. Choice narrows while the experience feels subjective. Consumers believe they are unique, but they are behaving according to data patterns.

The illusion of choice also shifts responsibility. When consumers are regarded as free decision-makers, the system avoids accountability. Environmental damage is blamed on "consumer choice"; inequality is explained as "wrong choices." Systemic constraints are rendered invisible, and the moral burden is placed on the individual. Consumerism uses freedom to distribute guilt and obligation, leading people to optimize personal choices rather than question the system.

This illusion has significant political implications. When citizenship is replaced by consumption, democratic participation weakens. People turn to "ethical shopping" rather than collective action for social change. Language like "vote with your wallet" reinforces the idea that the market is the ultimate decision-making space. But wallet-based voting is inherently unequal—those with more money wield more "choice." In this way, the illusion of choice does not empower democracy; it quietly hollows it out.

The most profound and dangerous transformation of consumerism is that it does not merely sell things—it makes human identity itself marketable. When consumption progresses from need to desire, and desire to choice, the next logical step is the commodification of identity. At this stage, products no longer serve just functional or pleasure-based purposes; they become carriers of self-image, social standing, and even existential meaning. Individuals no longer ask, "What do I need?" but instead, "Who am I—and how will others perceive me?" Consumerism provides a market-friendly answer to this question.

Historically, identity was shaped through community, profession, philosophy, or lived experience. People constructed their sense of self through relationships, actions, and values. In modern consumer societies, identity increasingly expresses itself through external symbols—brands, lifestyles, aesthetics, and consumption patterns. This produces a crucial shift: identity becomes performed rather than lived. What is visible is considered real. Consumerism simplifies this performance: "Buy this, and become this."

The market has categorized identity into manageable labels: successful, minimalist, rebel, conscious, luxury-lover, spiritual, intellectual, fitness-focused. Each category carries associated products, brands, and visual codes. Consumers feel they are expressing individuality, but in reality, they are selecting pre-designed identity packages. This process frees individuals from complex self-reflection—identity creation is outsourced to the market. Individuality becomes an illusion operating through mass-produced templates.

A key psychological effect of this commodification is that self-worth becomes tethered to consumption. When identity is linked to products, validation comes through the market. Social approval, respect, and belonging become accessible only to those who can afford visible markers of identity. People begin to see their value not as intrinsic but as exchangeable. Failure to meet market standards leads to feelings of inadequacy, internalized as personal failure, though it is structurally produced.

Digital culture intensifies this identity-for-sale dynamic. Social media platforms become marketplaces where the self is continuously curated, edited, and displayed. Likes, followers, and engagement metrics quantify identity. People do not only consume—they present themselves to be consumed. The boundary between consumer and product blurs; the self becomes a brand. Self-branding is a natural extension of capitalist logic, where everything—including personality—possesses monetizable potential.

The social impact of identity commodification is profound. When identity is market-driven, social relations become transactional. Connections are no longer built on values or shared experiences but on status symbols and consumption signals. Alienation rises as people evaluate each other instead of understanding one another. Comparison culture amplifies this alienation, since every identity is public and measurable. Individuals constantly feel ahead or behind, normalizing anxiety and dissatisfaction.

Philosophically, identity-for-sale generates an existential crisis. When the self is defined by external objects, it becomes inherently unstable. Products become outdated, trends shift, and market expectations change. The consumer self is never settled, always under pressure to update, upgrade, and rebrand. The system justifies this instability as "self-improvement," but in reality, it creates a permanent state of insecurity that sustains consumption.

Consumerism's most practical and damaging outcome emerges when desire transforms into economic obligation. At this stage, consumerism teaches not just wanting but paying, working, and staying bound. Debt, credit systems, EMIs, and lifestyle loans are not accidental by-products—they are structural tools. Their purpose is simple: to lock the consumer into the system from present to future. Debt converts consumption from a momentary act into long-term discipline.

Historically, debt was a necessity—used for famine, medical emergencies, or survival crises. Modern consumer capitalism normalizes and moralizes debt. Today, debt is not a sign of failure but a marker of "responsible adulthood." Credit cards, buy-now-pay-later schemes, and zero-interest EMIs tie consumption to instant gratification while pledging the consumer's future labor.

Debt makes work compulsory rather than optional. Loans, EMIs, and lifestyle commitments turn employment into a mechanism for repayment rather than mere survival. Consumers tolerate job exploitation or dissatisfaction because economic pressure constrains them. Debt becomes a silent tool of labor discipline—no external authority or law is required; debt itself is sufficient.

The work–consume–repeat cycle normalizes dependency. Consumers are taught that work's reward is consumption: a new phone, a better lifestyle, an upgraded identity. But rewards are never stable. Satisfying one desire triggers another, often more expensive. Income growth competes with consumption growth, but satisfaction never catches up. Consumers are trapped in a perpetual chase; the system does not want complete and content individuals, only motivated, anxious, indebted ones.

Debt also controls time and future choices. Loans narrow options for risk-taking, creative exploration, political dissent, or alternative lifestyles. Consumers default to "safe" decisions because the cost of deviation is high. Consumerism rewards conformity and punishes deviation. Theoretically, freedom exists, but practically, it is unaffordable—a central contradiction of consumer society.

The psychological impact of debt is severe. Continuous financial pressure generates anxiety, guilt, and self-blame. Consumers internalize economic stress as personal incompetence rather than systemic entrapment. This internalization serves the system perfectly: instead of questioning it, people optimize themselves—better budgeting, productivity, and hustle. Structural exploitation is disguised as self-improvement, while the system remains untouched.

Debt also has broad social implications. When large populations operate under debt, collective resistance weakens. Indebted people become cautious, compliant, and risk-averse. Strikes, protests, and systemic challenges become costly. Debt thus functions not only as an economic tool but also as a political stabilizer. Consumerism does not openly suppress democracy—it keeps people too busy, constrained, and preoccupied for dissent to seem practical.

Globally, this logic is even starker. In developing economies, consumerism penetrates through aspiration and takes root through debt. Middle classes are sold the dream of a "global lifestyle," while wages and social security fail to keep pace. The result is chronic stress, overwork, and normalized exhaustion. The system celebrates this exhaustion as productivity and ambition. Burnout is rebranded as a badge of honor. This is the brutal irony of consumer capitalism: the system tires people out, then sells them the solutions to the fatigue it created.

The most underestimated impact of consumerism is not economic or material, but psychological and cultural. When desire is continuously stimulated, choice is turned into an illusion, and identity is tied to the market, the inevitable outcome is a mentally exhausted and culturally hollow society. Consumerism promises prosperity and comfort, but the actual result is often anxiety, dissatisfaction, and emotional emptiness. This contradiction is not accidental; it is a natural consequence of the internal logic of consumer society.

At the psychological level, consumerism normalizes a permanent state of dissatisfaction. Consumers are taught that fulfillment will come with the next purchase, the next upgrade, or the next achievement. The present moment is never enough. Individuals become constantly future-oriented: “When I get this, I will be happy.” But as soon as one moment arrives, the system immediately introduces the next desire. In this endless cycle of anticipation, satisfaction is short-lived and fleeting, while craving is permanent. This state normalizes anxiety and restlessness. Consumers perceive their unease as an individual weakness, when in reality it is a systemically produced mental condition.

Comparison culture is a central driver of this psychological cost. Consumerism sells the narrative of individuality and uniqueness, but in practice enforces constant comparison. Through social media and advertising, people continuously see curated, idealized lives—better bodies, better homes, better relationships, better success stories. The cumulative effect of this exposure is that individuals always feel lesser than someone else. Self-worth becomes relative, permanently destabilizing mental peace. In this culture, confidence does not grow naturally; it comes from temporary validation, which then demands repeated consumption.

Culturally, consumerism erodes traditional sources of meaning-making. Previously, people derived meaning through values, philosophies, art, community practices, and shared narratives. In consumer society, meaning is not replaced but outsourced—through brand narratives, lifestyle goals, and aspirational images. Life’s purpose no longer revolves around personal growth or collective well-being; it becomes about “keeping up” and “staying relevant.” This shift causes culture to lose depth. Symbols and rituals become hollow because their reference point is the market, not lived experience.

Consumerism also deeply impacts relationships. When self-worth and identity are defined through consumption, human relationships subtly become transactional. People are evaluated, consciously or unconsciously, based on their status signals, lifestyle markers, and utility. Friendship, love, and social bonding start to depend more on presentation and compatibility of lifestyles than on authenticity. This transactional orientation weakens intimacy, as genuine connection requires vulnerability and presence, which are discouraged in a fast-paced, performance-driven consumer environment.

Mental health issues such as anxiety, depression, and burnout are disproportionately high in consumer societies. The cause is not just work pressure or technology, but existential fatigue—a kind of exhaustion that occurs when life has no stable meaning anchor. Consumerism keeps people busy but unfulfilled. There is constant pressure to achieve, upgrade, and display. Against this pressure, rest, stillness, and contentment are portrayed as laziness or lack of ambition. Psychological recovery spaces are made morally suspect.

Cultural imagination also shrinks under consumerism. When every problem's solution is imagined as a product, alternative ways of living—collective care, simplicity, non-market creativity—appear unrealistic or impractical. Consumerism constrains imagination; it only presents futures that are achievable through the market. This results in people stopping thinking outside the system.

Another important psychological effect is self-alienation. When individuals derive their desires from market cues, they gradually disconnect from their inner voice. They cannot recognize what they genuinely want—rest, connection, creativity, purpose—because the system has already given them a ready-made syllabus for desire. This alienation is treated as "confusion" or "lack of motivation," while in reality, it is a structural outcome.

Culturally, consumerism produces a society that is surface-rich but depth-poor. There is an abundance of aesthetics, trends, and novelty, but wisdom, patience, and long-term thinking are scarce. Art becomes mostly content—quickly consumable, algorithm-friendly, and disposable. Knowledge is viewed through the lens of utility: will it make money? Will it help my career? Within this framework, philosophical, ethical, and existential inquiry becomes marginal, as it does not promise immediate returns.

Consumerism's environmental impact is often presented as a "side effect"—pollution, climate change, and resource depletion as unfortunate but manageable consequences. A deeper analysis shows that ecological destruction is not a by-product but a structural outcome. A system based on endless consumption cannot be sustainable on a finite planet. Consumerism's core logic—produce more, sell more, replace faster—directly conflicts with nature's basic limits. Therefore, the environmental crisis is not an accidental failure, but the logical result of consumer society's design.

Consumerism drives production not according to need but according to volatile desire. Desires are unstable, so production must continuously expand and accelerate. Natural resources are treated as "inputs"—forests as raw material, rivers as waste channels, the atmosphere as a dumping ground. Nature's value is not intrinsic but extractive and utilitarian. Anything that is not useful for the market is expendable. This worldview is the opposite of environmental ethics.

Overproduction is the ecological engine of consumerism. Products are made not because people need them, but because the market must grow. Overproduction directly results in massive waste—clothes that are never worn, gadgets that quickly become obsolete, packaging that serves advertising more than use. Planned obsolescence is central here: products are intentionally designed with a short lifespan. Replacement cycles accelerate, and the extraction–production–disposal loop intensifies.

Climate change is consumerism's most visible ecological consequence. Fossil fuel-dependent global supply chains, fast logistics, and energy-intensive lifestyles normalize greenhouse gas emissions. Consumer society presents convenience as a virtue—fast delivery, disposable goods, constant availability—but the ecological cost is invisible. Carbon footprints are turned into individual responsibilities, while systemic consumption patterns remain untouched. This narrative shifts guilt onto consumers, letting the system remain intact.

Consumerism also drives biodiversity loss. Land clearing for agriculture, mining, infrastructure, and urban expansion destroys species' habitats. Yet, the consumer narrative justifies this destruction as "development" and "progress." When consumption growth becomes the ultimate indicator of success, ecological stability becomes a secondary concern. Species extinction is reduced to an unfortunate statistic, rather than an irreversible loss of life systems. Non-human life becomes nearly invisible outside the market framework.

Another critical issue is waste colonialism. Consumer societies export their waste—plastics, electronics, toxic materials—to Global South regions. This unevenly distributes ecological burden. Wealthy consumers enjoy clean environments, while marginalized communities face pollution, health hazards, and environmental degradation. Consumerism here produces not just ecological, but ethical injustice—a global extension of inequality, where consumption's pleasures are concentrated in one place and destruction occurs elsewhere.

Green consumerism is often presented as a solution—eco-friendly products, sustainable brands, ethical consumption. But this approach does not fundamentally address the problem. As long as the core logic of endless consumption remains, "green choices" are only aesthetic adjustments. Sustainable packaging combined with overconsumption remains unsustainable. Green consumerism does not challenge the system; it gives consumers the feeling of responsibility while production and growth structures remain unchanged. It is moral outsourcing of the ecological crisis.

Consumerism's most dangerous ecological impact is its denial of limits. Planetary boundaries—finite resources, regenerative capacity, ecological balance—become inconvenient truths in market narratives. Consumer culture discounts the future and prioritizes immediate gratification. This short-termism leads to long-term ecological collapse. Climate tipping points, water scarcity, soil degradation—these warnings are drowned out by consumer society's noise. The promise of growth frames acknowledging limits as weakness.

Philosophically, consumerism fundamentally distorts humans' relationship with nature. People begin to see themselves not as part of the ecosystem but as its manager and exploiter. Nature becomes a backdrop—for Instagram aesthetics or resource extraction. This alienation makes ecological destruction emotionally distant. When there is no connection, care is superficial. The environmental crisis only seems urgent when it directly disrupts lifestyle.

Modern consumer society projects itself as the most advanced form of freedom. We are told that we are the freest people in history—we can buy what we want, wear what we want, watch what we want, and design our lives according to our preferences. At the center of this narrative is choice. But when this choice is critically analyzed, it becomes clear that the freedom displayed under consumerism is largely illusory—a carefully curated freedom that exists only within the system's boundaries.

Consumerism redefines freedom. We generally understand freedom as "being able to do whatever one wishes," but the problem begins here, because we do not choose our desires, fears, ambitions, or background. Where we are born—family, class, culture, economic condition—is predetermined. Absolute free will is an illusion.

In the present capitalist world, the meaning of freedom is even more distorted. Capitalism defines freedom as market choice—you can choose your job, select brands, pick your lifestyle. On the surface, all this appears as freedom, but in reality, it is only choice among pre-set options, not freedom to go beyond the system. When not working leads to hunger, homelessness, or social exclusion, choice ceases to be genuine—it becomes compulsion. Capitalism creates desires—through ads, media, and social comparison—and then claims, "See, you are free, go buy."

This illusion is closely linked with democracy as well. In a consumer society, citizens are gradually converted into consumer-citizens. Political participation is reduced to voting, while market logic overlays democracy: just as products compete in the market, political parties and ideologies are "sold." Election campaigns become performances, slogans behave like brands, and leaders are marketed as influencers.

The most dangerous effect of consumerism is that it diffuses political dissatisfaction through consumption. If you are frustrated by job insecurity, inequality, or social injustice, the system channels this frustration into retail therapy, entertainment, and shopping. Streaming platforms, gadgets, and lifestyle upgrades act as psychological safety valves, while structural problems remain intact.

Choice becomes central again. Consumer society continuously tells us that we are free because we can choose. But the origin of these choices is rarely questioned. Desires are not spontaneous; they are manufactured, amplified, and normalized. When you "choose" something that has already been recommended by an algorithm, glorified by advertising, and normalized by social pressure, how autonomous is this choice? Consumerism converts freedom into an internal experience—"I feel free"—while the roots of that feeling lie in external power structures.

This also affects democratic equality. Market-based freedom is inherently unequal because purchasing power is uneven. The wealthy consumer has more choices—better education, healthcare, lifestyle, and influence—while freedom for the poor remains largely theoretical. Yet consumer ideology insists that everyone is equal because "the market is open to all." Inequality is thus framed as individual failure rather than systemic injustice. The promise of democracy—political equality—is silently eroded under market logic.

Consumerism presents itself as a neutral economic behavior—as if it were just an advanced form of buying and selling. But a critical analysis reveals that it is a totalizing system that shapes not only markets but human consciousness, identity, and social relations. The system does not merely sell products; it sells meaning, belonging, and purpose—and in doing so, it redefines the individual within the logic of the market.

Consumerism has transformed identity from an internal process into an external performance. People now understand themselves less through "Who am I?" and more through "What do I own?" The most serious consequence of this shift is that self-worth becomes volatile, fluctuating with market trends. Such an identity can never be stable because the market's very function is to create change. Anxiety, comparison, and emptiness are therefore not accidental side effects of consumer society; they are its structural outcomes.

When Faith Becomes a Cage

One of the most distinctive features of '*Homo sapiens*' is not our physical strength, speed, or even our raw intelligence in problem-solving. What truly sets us apart from every other species is our ability to imagine, to create fictions, and to make large groups of people believe in them. This capacity is often called the '*Cognitive Revolution*', which occurred roughly 70,000 years ago. During this period, humans developed the neurological ability to form complex language, abstract concepts, and shared myths.

Most animals can communicate about immediate realities. A chimpanzee, for example, can signal that there is a lion nearby or that a certain fruit tree is full of ripe figs. But it cannot communicate that "the lion is the guardian spirit of our clan" or "if we all respect this tree, our tribe will prosper." Only humans can invent and transmit such imagined realities. This unique psychological ability to believe in stories that do not exist in the physical world—whether gods, nations, money, or laws—is what enabled large-scale cooperation among strangers. Religion is one of the earliest and most powerful expressions of this cognitive capacity.

In the earliest hunter-gatherer societies, religion took the form of animism. Animism is the belief that every element of nature—rivers, mountains, trees, animals—has a spirit or consciousness. This worldview made sense in small, nomadic communities where survival depended on close observation of the environment.

If a group of hunters failed to catch deer for several days, they might explain it by saying that the spirit of the deer was angry. If a storm destroyed their camp, they might conclude that the river or the mountain spirit was displeased. Such explanations were not irrational in their historical context. Rather, they provided a psychological framework for understanding uncertainty and danger in a complex world.

Psychologically, animism satisfied a deep human tendency called agent detection—our brain's habit of attributing agency or intention to natural phenomena. For survival, it is better to mistakenly assume a rustle in the bushes is a predator than to dismiss it and be eaten. This same bias encouraged early humans to see intentional spirits behind natural events. Over thousands of years, this evolved into fully developed animistic religions.

With the '*Agricultural Revolution*', about 12,000 years ago, humans settled in permanent villages, domesticated plants and animals, and built larger communities. Social structures became more complex, and so did belief systems. Instead of countless spirits inhabiting every rock and tree, people began to conceptualize specialized gods who controlled specific aspects of life.

A god of fertility could bless the harvest, a god of rain could bring monsoon, and a god of war could protect the tribe from enemies. This was the birth of polytheism. Polytheism reflected the realities of early agrarian societies: just as society had specialized roles—farmers, soldiers, rulers—so too did the divine realm.

Polytheism also made political sense. Different communities could merge their pantheons, recognizing each other's gods rather than rejecting them. When two tribes united, instead of fighting over whose god was true, they could agree that both sets of gods existed. This flexibility made polytheism one of the most enduring religious systems in history, surviving in forms as diverse as ancient Sumerian/Mesopotamian Mythology, Egyptian Mythology etc.

Over time, however, some cultures moved from polytheism to monotheism—the belief in one supreme God. This was not an inevitable step, but a radical transformation. Instead of many deities with divided powers, a single God was imagined as the universal ruler of the cosmos.

Monotheism offered both simplicity and power. By claiming that one God was the source of all truth and morality, it created a unified moral order. But it also introduced exclusivity. In polytheism, your god and my god could coexist. In monotheism, if one God is true, then all others must be false. This shift intensified religious conflict, as followers of different monotheistic traditions—Judaism, Christianity, Islam—fought not merely for territory but for absolute truth.

Psychologically, monotheism satisfied the human need for order and coherence. A world governed by many capricious gods could feel chaotic, but a world ruled by one supreme being seemed structured and purposeful. At the same time, this worldview provided rulers with a powerful tool: kings and emperors could claim divine authority, presenting their rule as the will of the one true God.

Early religions, whether animistic or polytheistic, were usually local. They belonged to a specific tribe, culture, or region. But as empires expanded and trade networks grew, there arose universal religions—belief systems that claimed their truths applied to all humans, regardless of birthplace or ethnicity.

Christianity, and Islam are prime examples. They spread not only through conquest but also through trade, migration, and missionary work. These religions promised salvation or liberation to anyone who believed, creating spiritual communities that transcended local identities.

Religion also justified social hierarchies. Kings claimed divine right, priests controlled rituals, and caste or class divisions were presented as ordained by the gods. In this way, religion stabilized unequal systems of power, making them appear natural and eternal.

Modern psychology helps explain why religion was so compelling. Humans have several cognitive biases that make belief in the supernatural almost inevitable:

1. Agency detection bias – We assume that events have intentional causes. This makes gods and spirits a natural explanation for storms, diseases, or crop failures.

2. Theory of mind – Our ability to imagine what others are thinking allows us to also imagine what invisible beings might think. If I can guess my neighbor's motives, I can also guess the motives of the rain god.

3. Pattern-seeking – Humans hate randomness. We prefer to see meaningful patterns, even when none exist. Religion offered comforting narratives for unpredictable events.

4. Fear of death – Religion provided answers about life after death, reducing existential anxiety and making individuals more willing to sacrifice for the group.

These psychological tendencies made religion deeply "sticky" in the human brain. Even today, when scientific explanations exist, many people still intuitively lean toward supernatural thinking because it resonates with these ancient cognitive shortcuts.

Seen through a scientific lens, religion is best understood not as revelation from the heavens but as a product of the human mind—our cognitive architecture, our psychological needs, and our social structures. It gave meaning to a chaotic world, provided moral rules, and justified power systems. It helped humans move from small bands of hunter-gatherers to massive civilizations and empires.

This also implies that religion is not eternal. Just as animism gradually gave way to polytheism, and polytheism to monotheism, the belief systems of today are not final destinations. They too may eventually be replaced—giving way to new frameworks of meaning and belonging, shaped by future social conditions, knowledge systems, and human needs, perhaps in forms that are not yet imaginable.

The constant thread is not the gods themselves but the human ability to invent and collectively believe in shared fictions. That, more than anything else, is what makes us human.

What do you believe in, and why? Have you ever examined the roots of your deepest beliefs?

In our society, especially regarding religion, believing something without evidence is not only acceptable but is considered a virtue. It is called faith. But is it really a virtue, or is it a mental weakness that we have dressed up in the cloak of respect? Think about it: if a friend tells you that there is an invisible unicorn in their garden, what would you say? You would probably ask them for evidence. If they say there's no need for evidence and they just believe, you would start worrying about their mental health.

But when billions of people say the same about an invisible, all-powerful entity, we call it faith and respect it.

Belief—that is, accepting something as true without sufficient evidence—is a flaw in any field. So why does it become a virtue in the domain of religion? What is faith, really?

Faith is not just a harmless personal feeling. It is a mental framework that teaches us that some questions are wrong to ask. That doubting certain ideas is sinful. It tells us that some books are so sacred that every word in them must be taken literally as true, even if those words completely contradict modern science, logic, and morality.

Would you deposit your money in a bank that says, "We have no security system; just have faith in us"? Would you undergo surgery by a doctor who says, "I have never studied medicine, but I have faith that I can do it"? No, you wouldn't. Everywhere in life, you demand evidence, check qualifications, and use reason.

So why do we close the doors of reason when it comes to the most important questions of life, such as: How was the universe created? What is our purpose? What happens after death? Respecting faith is, in fact, disrespecting reason. It is a mental habit that prevents us from seeing the world as it is and forces us to see it as we wish it to be.

Now you might be wondering, what is the danger in this? If someone peacefully believes something at home, how does it harm others? But our beliefs shape our actions. What we believe is what we do.

If a person believes that a particular book says non-believers must be destroyed, this is no longer just an idea—it becomes a dangerous ideology that can lead to violence. If someone believes prayer alone can cure illness and does not take their child to a doctor, their faith can cost the child's life.

When we glorify irrational processes like faith, we open a door through which all kinds of dangerous and absurd ideas take root in society. We lose the ability to separate good ideas from bad ones because our standard is no longer evidence but the power of specific belief.

Imagine two people: one believes God promised him a holy land, and the other believes the same God promised him the same land. Each has their own holy book to back their claim. How will they resolve this dispute? Not through reason and evidence, because the nature of their belief is beyond logic. They cannot have a conversation; they can only repeat their beliefs, and when dialogue ends, violence begins.

Religion traps us in the cages of different beliefs, from which we cannot reach each other. It prevents us from standing on a shared reality, a common ground of reason. In a world with nuclear weapons, such a situation can be extremely destructive.

Isn't the root of many of the world's problems this habit of believing without evidence? Are we honoring a mental wiring that pits us against each other? But has faith always been so destructive, or did history do something that turned faith into a weapon? What events made humans act inhumanely in the name of faith?

History is soaked in blood in the name of religion and faith. This is not an exaggeration but a bitter truth. The argument is that religious violence is not a deviation or misinterpretation of religion but a direct and logical consequence of many religious texts.

When you teach people that a book is the infallible word of God and that it says anyone who does not believe like you is wicked, sinful, and must be punished, you are preparing an ideological ground for violence. It's like pouring petrol on a dry grass heap and hoping no spark will ignite it.

Let's take a few steps back in history. Recall the Christian Crusades or religious wars. These were not just struggles for land; they were holy wars blessed by the Pope.

Thousands of soldiers and ordinary people set out to attack other countries believing that they were fulfilling God's will. They believed that killing infidels was a virtuous act that would grant them entry into paradise. They massacred countless innocent people, including women and children, all in the name of their religion.

Then consider the Spanish Inquisition, where the Church systematically tortured and burned alive those suspected of heresy. What was their crime? Their crime was questioning the teachings of the Church or thinking differently. They were forced through extreme suffering to admit that they were worshippers of Satan, all in the name of saving their souls.

Where does the inspiration for such cruelty come from? This inspiration comes from religious doctrines that teach that faith is so important that taking a life for it is justified. And this is not just a thing of the past. The attackers of 9/11 (2001) were neither fools nor mad. By their own standards, they were acting rationally. They genuinely believed they were participating in a jihad, that death would reward them with 72 virgins in paradise, and that by punishing what they saw as "evil," such as America, they were pleasing Allah and fulfilling divine will. Every step they took was inspired by their religious belief. They did not fear death because their faith taught them that death is a gateway to a better life.

Until we accept that their faith inspired them to do this, we will never reach the root of the problem. We will keep looking for answers in external causes like poverty, politics, or American foreign policy, while the real cause lies in the ideas present in their minds—ideas that their faith has made sacred and unquestionable.

Are all religions equally dangerous? No. Some religious texts and doctrines explicitly encourage violence and intolerance more than others. A religion whose sacred book teaches love for one's enemies cannot be measured on the same scale as one whose book calls for war against non-believers. This does not mean one religion is "good" and the other "bad"; rather, some ideologies are more incompatible with the modern, multicultural, global world. It emphasizes that we must evaluate ideas based on their merits and flaws, not on how many people believe in them or how old they are. When an idea breeds violence, hatred, and division, we should not respect it merely because it is religious.

But here a deeper question arises. Many people will say this only applies to extremists. Ordinary peaceful religious people are not like this. Yet, ordinary liberal believers unknowingly act as a shield for extremists. How? Because they keep alive in society the idea that faith should be respected. They create an atmosphere where questioning or criticizing religion is seen as rude or improper. In this climate of respect, extremist ideologies also flourish, because they too are a form of faith. When you say that Jesus walked on water or Moses parted the sea, you leave a door open for irrationality. Then, when someone else claims that he believes in killing infidels, you have no strong rational basis to prove him wrong, because you yourself suspended the rules of reason.

So does this mean that there is nothing good in religion? Are morality, community, and meaning in life—all the positive things religion gives us—a deception? Do we really need religion for morality and peace of mind?

So far, we have looked at the dangerous aspects of faith and its bloody history. Hearing all this, a natural question arises: what about the good aspects of religion? Does religion not make us moral? Does it not give us comfort in difficult times and a sense of belonging to a community? Morality, love, compassion, and meaning in life are indeed good things, but do we need religion or God for them? The argument is not that religion has nothing good. The argument is that what is good in religion is not inherently religious. These qualities and emotions are part of human nature and can be obtained and cultivated without any supernatural belief.

Do we really need an ancient book to learn the difference between right and wrong? Do we need the fear of a God, threatening us with hell, to behave well toward others? Absolutely not. Do you believe that hurting a child is wrong? You would say yes, it is definitely wrong. Now the question is why is it wrong? Is it wrong because a sacred book says so, or because it causes tremendous pain to the child? For a rational and sensitive person, the answer is clear: it is wrong because we understand suffering. We can feel empathy, and we know that we ourselves would not want to experience such pain. The foundation of our morality is the understanding of the well-being of other beings, not adherence to some ancient command. Religion has hijacked morality. It has made us believe that without it, we would lose our moral compass, when the truth is that the foundation of morality lies in our shared human experience and reason.

Scandinavia (Norway, Sweden, Denmark) is largely atheist, yet has the world's lowest crime, highest equality, and strong welfare.

In contrast, highly religious states like Afghanistan, Nigeria, India, Pakistan, Yemen and Saudi Arabia are marked by violence, inequality, and repression.

Morality is not divine; it is human. It arises from empathy, cooperation, and reason.

In fact, religious morality can sometimes be unethical. For example, when a religion labels homosexuality as a sin or considers women inferior to men, it promotes suffering and discrimination, which is against any rational moral system.

Now let us talk about comfort and meaning in life. Many people say that religion gives them the strength to face life's hardships. The belief that a higher power is watching or that we will reunite with loved ones after death can certainly be comforting. Yes, it can be comforting. But should we live relying on comforting lies, or should we confront the harsh reality? Should a doctor tell a cancer patient, "Everything is fine, you are perfectly healthy," just because it feels good to hear it? No, that would be cruelty.

We should learn to accept reality in all its grandeur and complexity, instead of clinging to childish, false stories about the universe. The meaning of life does not come from some external source; we must create it ourselves. Our relationships, our work, art, science, the beauty of nature, helping others—all these can be sources of a meaningful life, and they require no supernatural belief.

What about the sense of community? Churches, mosques, and temples bring people together and give them a sense of belonging. That is true. But is it the only way to build a community? We can create strong, meaningful communities through sports clubs, book clubs, charitable organizations, scientific societies, and countless other ways. Religious communities often operate on an "us versus them" mentality, dividing people based on what they believe.

We need to trust our reason, our empathy, and our creativity. Once we understand that we do not depend on religion for these good things, we can more clearly see its dangerous and divisive aspects and feel free to reject them. But all of this involves reason and evidence. There has always been tension between religion and science. Can they coexist, or is it a grand battle where only one can ultimately win?

Religion and science are two completely opposite and incompatible ways of reaching the truth. This is not a minor disagreement but a fundamental struggle to understand the nature of reality. On one side, there is science, which is based on observation, experimentation, evidence, and a continuous process of self-correction. On the other side, there is religion, which is based on revelations, ancient scriptures, and beliefs that cannot be altered. No real compromise is possible between the two.

Consider how science works. A scientist formulates a hypothesis and then gathers evidence to test it. If the evidence supports the hypothesis, it is provisionally accepted. If the evidence contradicts it, the hypothesis is modified or completely discarded. In science, no idea or theory is sacred. Newton's laws were refined by Einstein. Every theory is constantly challenged and can be changed based on better evidence. The strength of science lies in its humility—it acknowledges that we do not know everything and can be wrong. The goal of science is to obtain reliable knowledge about the universe—knowledge that works, allowing us to develop vaccines, send spacecraft into space, and create technologies like the internet.

Now look at how religion operates. Religion begins with a conclusion—one written in a sacred book or conveyed by a prophet. For example, the universe was created in six days, or a particular person was the son of God. These conclusions are considered absolute truths. We do not know what the ultimate truth is, and it is entirely possible that we may never know it. Given this fundamental limitation of human knowledge, the most intellectually honest response is to acknowledge uncertainty rather than fill the gaps with comforting stories. Accepting "we do not know" requires far more courage and maturity than believing in an unverified narrative. When no conclusive evidence exists, inventing or inheriting a belief is not wisdom—it is an escape from uncertainty.

They are not allowed to be tested or challenged. If evidence arises that contradicts these beliefs—like fossil records or genetic studies supporting evolution—the faithful reject the evidence rather than their belief. The goal of religion is to preserve belief, no matter what. It is a mental state that says, "I do not care what the evidence says; I will believe this anyway."

Science encourages us to change our ideas about the world, while faith encourages us to turn away from reality. Many argue that science and religion occupy separate domains: science answers "how" questions—how the universe works—while religion answers "why" questions—what our purpose is. This idea is called Non-Overlapping Magisteria (NOMA). But this is a false and artificial division. Religion does not only claim to answer "why" questions; it also makes many claims about "how" the world works.

Virgin birth, walking on water, raising the dead, answered prayers—these are all factual claims about the physical world. These are claims that can be scientifically tested, and whenever such claims are tested, they are consistently found to be false. Religion continually encroaches into the domain of science, and when science proves it wrong, it retreats under the cover of metaphor or spiritual truth.

The clearest example of this epic struggle is the debate over the theory of evolution. Science has mountains of evidence showing that life evolved slowly over millions of years. We have fossils, DNA evidence, and we can even observe bacteria and viruses evolving before our eyes. On the other hand, some religious beliefs claim that humans were created directly by their so called religious god in their current form. Both claims cannot be true simultaneously. Either we evolved, or we were created.

When believers reject evolution, they are not merely rejecting a scientific fact—they are rejecting the entire process of reason and evidence. They are essentially saying that their ancient story is more important than every piece of evidence we have discovered. To assume that the religion into which one is born alone possesses the ultimate and absolute truth—while all others are merely wrong—is not just an error of judgment but a profound intellectual arrogance. Such a belief rests entirely on accident of birth rather than reason, evidence, or critical inquiry. If truth were truly absolute and self-evident, it would not depend on geography, family, or historical circumstance. Treating inherited belief as unquestionable truth reduces complex human traditions to tribal loyalty and turns serious philosophical questions into blind allegiance.

Critique of Nationalism

Among the many ideas and institutions that have caused the greatest bloodshed, division, and artificial barriers in human history, '*Nationalism*' stands at the top. Even today, this idea shapes the consciousness of billions of people. But is nationalism really a force for human progress? Or is it a myth we have blindly accepted—one for which we continue to pay the price in wars, partitions, and hatred?

In the earliest phases of civilization, there were no nations and no borders. Small tribes, clans, and villages were the basic social units. Identity was rooted in family, kinship, or local community.

With the '*Agricultural Revolution*' and permanent settlements, societies grew larger and more complex. From here came towns, city-states, and empires. But the nation as we understand it is a modern invention—born in 16th–17th century Europe with the rise of industrialization, printing technology, and modern administration.

Nationalism first tied language and culture to political power. "*One language, one people, one nation*" became the rallying cry in Europe. In the 18th and 19th centuries, nationalism often acted as a force against empires: Italy and Germany unified under its banner, and colonies across the world began to imagine independence. Yet the same idea quickly mutated into a doctrine of ethnic superiority, racial hatred, and imperial wars.

The 20th century saw nationalism at its most extreme in fascism and Nazism. Hitler built the myth of an "*Aryan nation*," which justified the extermination of millions of Jews, Roma, and others. Nationalism drove the Second World War, the deadliest conflict in human history. At the same time, nationalist politics in India led to Partition, uprooting millions and killing hundreds of thousands.

Today, in the 21st century, when humanity faces global challenges like climate change, pandemics, and technological interdependence, nationalism still pushes people into the *"us versus them"* trap.

The human brain has a deep tendency to seek group identity. In early tribes, belonging to a collective meant survival. We feel comfortable with those who are like us and suspicious of those who are different. This *"ingroup vs outgroup"* bias is the psychological root of nationalism.

Nationalism also gives people meaning and pride. Saying *"I am a citizen of this nation"* makes an individual feel part of something vast, powerful, and glorious. Elites and ruling classes amplify this sentiment, using it to maintain order and justify power.

Social psychology explains this through social identity theory: people construct their self-image by comparing themselves to others. If my nation is great, then I too am great. This is why people grow so emotional about flags, anthems, or armies—even when their daily lives are shaped by poverty, injustice, or exploitation.

Nationalism is not only born from history and politics; it is also carefully manufactured through culture, education, and mass communication. Human beings are not naturally born with national identity. A child enters the world without knowledge of borders, flags, or anthems. These symbols and emotions must be taught, repeated, and embedded into the mind until they become "*common sense*." The mechanisms through which nationalism becomes normalized are propaganda and mass psychology. Schools, mass media, and cinema play central roles in this process, creating emotional conditioning that makes loyalty to the nation appear natural, unquestionable, and even sacred.

From the earliest years of formal education, schools act as factories for producing national identity. History textbooks are written not as objective records but as patriotic narratives. Victories are celebrated, defeats are reinterpreted as moral triumphs, and complexities are erased to create a clear picture of "*us versus them*."

This process is not accidental. States deliberately design curricula to shape young minds. By teaching children that their nation has a glorious past, a unique destiny, and sacred symbols, schools create citizens who internalize nationalism as part of their identity. Questioning the nation becomes unthinkable because the narrative is presented as truth, not ideology. Ingroup–outgroup psychology is reinforced as children learn to admire national heroes while distrusting or demonizing outsiders. The classroom thus becomes the first site of nationalist propaganda.

While schools establish nationalism in childhood, mass media continually reinforces it in adulthood. Newspapers, radio, television, and digital platforms constantly reproduce the idea of the nation through language and imagery. Headlines declare national victories or humiliations: "*India Defeats Pakistan in Cricke*t," "*China Launches Moon Mission*," "*America Leads the World in Innovation*." Even neutral events are narrated through national frames, as if every achievement or failure must be understood in terms of national pride.

Media also constructs enemies. News outlets amplify threats from "*foreign rivals,*" framing conflicts in nationalist terms. During wars, journalists act as cheerleaders, glorifying "*our soldiers*" while demonizing the other side. In peacetime, economic competition is presented as a struggle between nations rather than between companies or systems. Through repetition, citizens learn to interpret world events as contests between nations.

Propaganda does not always take the form of overt lies. More often, it works through selection and emphasis. Stories that glorify the nation are highlighted; those that question it are buried. Failures are framed as temporary setbacks, while successes are magnified into proof of national greatness. Over time, the constant background noise of patriotic news normalizes nationalism as the default way of understanding reality.

Cinema has always been more than entertainment; it has been one of the most effective dream machines for manufacturing nationalism. Unlike textbooks or speeches, which require conscious attention, cinema works directly on the senses and emotions. Its images, sounds, and narratives bypass rational analysis and sink into the subconscious, producing powerful emotional associations. Through cinema, nationalism is not merely thought—it is felt in the body.

The role of cinema in spreading propaganda is well documented. In Nazi Germany, Leni Riefenstahl's Triumph of the Will transformed Hitler's rallies into cinematic spectacles, making fascism appear not only legitimate but majestic and inevitable. In the Soviet Union, the doctrine of socialist realism turned cinema into a tool for glorifying workers, soldiers, and the "Motherland," weaving the myth of collective strength and sacrifice. In the United States, Hollywood has long reinforced American nationalism through war epics and military blockbusters—Top Gun, Saving

Private Ryan, and countless others—where America appears as the eternal defender of freedom and justice. The audience leaves the theater not only entertained but reaffirmed in national loyalty.

In India, cinema plays a particularly crucial role because film is one of the most accessible and influential cultural mediums in the country. Alongside patriotic war dramas such as Border or Uri: The Surgical Strike, which glorify sacrifice for the nation, a disturbing new trend has emerged: the deliberate production of propaganda films that distort history and demonize entire communities.

Certain filmmakers—most notably Vivek Agnihotri, director of The Kashmir Files and The Bengal Files —have turned cinema into a weapon of propaganda by presenting fabricated or exaggerated narratives. Muslims, in particular, are portrayed almost exclusively as villains, while Hindus are depicted as perpetual victims of atrocities.

This kind of cinema does not merely glorify nationalism; it manufactures communal hatred. By presenting one community as eternally evil and another as eternally persecuted, such films poison the social fabric. Instead of uniting citizens through shared human dignity, they deepen divisions, creating suspicion and hostility between neighbors. Worse, these films are not fringe productions; they are openly endorsed by political leaders and party's. Prime Minister Narendra Modi himself praised The Kashmir Files, signaling official approval of a film that promotes a one-sided, communal narrative. The ruling party, BJP, often encourages and amplifies such works because they serve its electoral strategy: fear and anger can be powerful tools for mobilizing votes.

Cinema's effectiveness lies in its ability to blur the line between fact and fiction. A film is consumed as an emotional experience; the audience weeps with the victims, rages at the villains, and feels catharsis in imagined justice. But when the villains are consistently portrayed as members of a real religious community, the emotions generated in the theater spill over into real life. Hatred, once entertained as fiction, becomes a political reality. This is why propaganda films are so dangerous: they can radicalize minds without the audience even realizing it.

Symbols amplify this effect. A flag waving in slow motion, soldiers marching to dramatic music, a mother weeping for her martyred son—these are not neutral images. They are carefully constructed emotional triggers. Combined with narratives of victimhood and revenge, they transform ordinary citizens into passionate defenders of an imagined nation under siege. The "sacred motherland" is portrayed as violated by villains, and the audience is invited to share in the outrage. Such cinematic conditioning makes blind loyalty to the state appear not only natural but moral.

The danger of this cinematic propaganda is not limited to politics; it corrodes the very foundations of society. When entire communities are demonized, social trust collapses. Violence becomes easier to justify, since the enemy has already been dehumanized on screen. When leaders endorse such films, they legitimize prejudice, presenting bigotry as patriotism. This is not a path toward unity or strength but toward endless division and violence.

Therefore, citizens must become critically aware of how cinema manipulates emotions. Films should be appreciated as art and storytelling, but audiences must ask: whose story is being told, and whose is being silenced? What emotions are being provoked, and for whose benefit? True national strength lies not in demonizing minorities or rewriting history but in facing reality with honesty and striving for justice for all. Cinema has the power to inspire compassion and solidarity, but in the hands of propagandists, it becomes a weapon of division.

If society remains uncritical, propaganda films will continue to spread like intoxicants, feeding hatred while distracting from real issues such as poverty, inequality, unemployment, and ecological collapse. Just as citizens must resist the addictive highs of nationalist pride, they must also resist the seductions of cinematic propaganda. A mature society does not confuse entertainment with truth, nor does it allow leaders to exploit films as tools for political gain. Only through awareness and critical thinking can cinema serve its highest purpose: not the glorification of myths, but the illumination of reality.

What unites schools, media, and cinema is their reliance on emotional repetition. National symbols—flags, anthems, monuments—are repeated until they become triggers for automatic responses. Seeing the flag can make the heart race, hearing the anthem can bring tears, watching soldiers march can evoke pride. These are not natural emotions; they are conditioned responses, built through years of exposure.

Psychologists have compared nationalism to religious devotion. Just as rituals, hymns, and sacred symbols create loyalty to a faith, national rituals create loyalty to the state. The difference is that nationalism is often invisible, presented not as belief but as reality. People say, "I am Indian" or "I am American" not as an opinion but as a fact, forgetting that the very categories of "India" or "America" are historical constructions. Propaganda works best when it hides itself.

The genius of nationalist propaganda is that it makes nationalism appear normal, even natural. People assume that loving one's nation is as obvious as loving one's family. They forget that the nation is an imagined community, not a biological reality. Schools, media, and cinema create this illusion of normality by embedding nationalism into everyday life.

Consider sporting events. International matches are presented as battles of nations, with fans waving flags and singing anthems. The joy of victory and the pain of defeat are experienced as collective emotions of the nation. Yet the players are individuals, the teams are corporations, and the event is organized by global institutions. Only propaganda makes it seem like the fate of the nation is at stake.

The same is true of consumer goods. Campaigns like "Buy American" or "Make in India" turn ordinary purchases into patriotic acts. A car or a smartphone becomes a symbol of national pride. Advertising agencies deliberately use national symbols to sell products, transforming consumption into political loyalty.

The normalization of nationalism through propaganda has dangerous consequences. Citizens are less likely to question wars, surveillance, or inequality when these are framed as patriotic necessities. Dissenters are branded as traitors, since loyalty to the nation is equated with morality itself. Propaganda thus suppresses critical thought and enforces conformity.

Moreover, propaganda amplifies hostility toward outsiders. When media and cinema constantly portray foreign nations as threats, citizens internalize suspicion and hatred. This makes conflicts more likely, since leaders can easily mobilize support for aggression by appealing to national pride.

Finally, propaganda distracts from real issues. Citizens obsessed with flags, borders, and imagined enemies often ignore poverty, inequality, and ecological collapse. Leaders exploit this by using nationalist rhetoric to deflect criticism of their failures. The emotional power of propaganda becomes a shield for corruption and injustice.

Understanding the role of propaganda reveals that nationalism is not natural but artificial. It shows that loyalty to the nation is not a biological instinct but a conditioned response.

Nationalism institutionalized "us vs them." It marginalized minorities, justified racism and ethnic cleansing, and turned wars into "holy crusades of patriotism." It provided moral cover for imperialism, colonization, and genocide.

World Wars I & II – Nationalist fervor and imperial ambitions killed tens of millions.

Partition of India (1947) – Religious-national identities tore apart communities, causing massacres and the displacement of millions.

Balkan Wars (1990s) – Ethnic nationalism led to genocide in the heart of Europe.

Rwanda Genocide (1994) – Hutu vs. Tutsi identities, inflamed by political nationalism, unleashed mass slaughter.

Modern cases – Trump's "America First," Modi's Hindu nationalism, Brexit's "British sovereignty," and Putin's "Russian glory" all weaken global cooperation while fueling internal hatred and external conflict.

In today's world, nationalism has no rational justification left.

1. Global problems demand global solutions. Climate crisis, pandemics, nuclear risk—these cannot be solved within borders. Nationalism blocks cooperation.

2. Economic interdependence. Supply chains, trade, and technology are deeply interconnected. Nationalism disrupts them.

3. Moral perspective. Why should a human life be valued less simply because it belongs to "another nation"? That is ethically absurd.

4. Artificial borders. National boundaries are accidents of history, not natural realities. They divide humanity.

5. A weapon of power. Nationalism has always been used by elites to justify war, propaganda, and exploitation.

One of the most striking ways to understand nationalism is to view it not merely as an ideology but as a form of addiction. Like alcohol, gambling, or drugs, nationalism produces powerful emotional highs while inflicting long-term harm. It gives people an intoxicating sense of belonging, power, and purpose, but these feelings are temporary, unstable, and often destructive. Leaders exploit this addictive quality to control populations, while citizens repeatedly return to the emotional "fix" of national pride, even when it damages their own well-being.

From a psychological perspective, national pride activates the brain's reward system in much the same way as addictive substances. When people see their flag waving, hear their anthem, or watch their athletes win a competition, the brain releases dopamine and oxytocin—chemicals associated with pleasure, bonding, and reward. These chemicals create a sense of euphoria and unity, much like the buzz of alcohol or the thrill of gambling.

This explains why sporting victories or military parades evoke such intense emotions. People feel uplifted, proud, even tearful, as if they have personally achieved something. In reality, the achievement belongs to individuals or institutions far removed from the ordinary citizen. But the nationalist framing transforms these distant events into personal triumphs. The brain cannot distinguish between one's own accomplishment and the symbolic victory of the nation. The result is a powerful but illusory high.

If nationalism is an addiction, then leaders act as dealers. They supply the emotional highs—military parades, fiery speeches, patriotic films—while profiting from citizens' dependence. By keeping populations hooked on national pride, leaders can distract from corruption, consolidate power, and justify policies that would otherwise face resistance.

For example, when governments face criticism for economic mismanagement, they often turn to nationalist spectacles. Wars, border tensions, or space missions are strategically emphasized to reignite patriotic fervor. The population, intoxicated by pride, rallies around the flag and forgets its grievances. The "rally-round-the-flag effect" is well documented: approval ratings for leaders often surge during wars or crises, regardless of policy failures. Nationalism functions as political anesthesia, dulling the pain of reality.

Addictions often create illusions. Alcohol makes a person feel confident and invincible, even as it impairs judgment. Nationalism creates a similar illusion at the collective level. Citizens feel that their nation is powerful, moral, and exceptional, even when evidence suggests otherwise.

Many Indians believe their country is destined to become a "Vishwaguru", even as millions lack access to basic education or healthcare. National pride intoxicates citizens with a false sense of greatness, preventing honest self-reflection.

Like all addictions, nationalism comes with heavy costs. Wars are the most obvious. Fueled by national pride, millions march to battlefields, convinced they are serving a sacred cause. The euphoria of victory or martyrdom blinds them to the destruction of human life.

Even in peacetime, nationalism erodes rational policy-making. Protectionist trade wars, wasteful military spending, and discriminatory laws are justified in the name of national pride. Citizens accept sacrifices—higher taxes, fewer freedoms, harsher laws—because they are framed as patriotic duties. The long-term damage accumulates: economies stagnate, societies polarize, minorities suffer persecution. Yet the addiction persists because the short-term emotional high outweighs the long-term harm in the minds of citizens.

School textbooks tell us a neat and comforting story: that on 15 August 1947, India achieved freedom. The tricolour was raised, the anthem was sung, and the people of India entered a new dawn. This narrative is repeated in classrooms, films, speeches, and commemorations every year. But is it the full truth—or merely a beautiful lie crafted to soothe our collective conscience!

The British did not design Indian institutions for public welfare. They designed them to maintain control. The police, courts, prisons, and bureaucracy were not instruments of justice or democracy but of surveillance, punishment, and fear. The colonial state's intention was not to empower Indians but to discipline them.

Michel Foucault, in Discipline and Punish, argues that modern systems of law and punishment are not merely about crime and justice—they are psychological weapons designed to keep populations obedient. Colonial India exemplified this principle. Laws were framed in an alien language, enforced through fear, and designed to break dissent.

What changed after 1947? The faces behind the desks, the uniforms, and the seats of power. But the structure, the mindset, and the methods remained intact. The very machinery built to protect British interests was preserved, merely repurposed to serve the Indian elite.

Consider the story of a Kolkata postal worker, "Binalal Sen" accused of stealing less than 100 rupees. In today's terms, it is a trivial amount—less than the cost of a single restaurant meal. Yet his case dragged on in court for 29 years. By the time the judgment arrived, he had lost his job, his family, and the best years of his life. The case itself became a form of punishment.

This is not an isolated story. Journalist P. Sainath, in Everybody Loves a Good Drought, documented hundreds of such cases where the poor and middle class entered courts seeking justice, only to discover that the judicial process itself was their punishment. For them, the court was not a refuge but a trap—a colonial design that survived independence.

If this system was built to empower the people, why does it continue to destroy lives? The truth is that the judiciary was never designed for the people. It was designed by the British to maintain order, to frighten, and to ensure that no challenge to authority could gain ground. Today, it serves the same function. The only difference is that the judges, lawyers, and officers are Indian. The architecture of fear remains unchanged.

Textbooks claim that independence brought democracy. But democracy is more than the right to vote. It is the ability to influence decisions, to participate in governance, and to hold power accountable. In India, democracy often appears more like theatre than reality.

Arundhati Roy, in The Algebra of Infinite Justice, described Indian democracy as an "event." On election day, the people are visible; their voices seem to matter. But the day after, they disappear again, reduced to passive spectators while decisions are taken in closed rooms by elites. This pattern mirrors the colonial practice of forming councils and boards that claimed to represent Indians but remained powerless in shaping real decisions.

Ramachandra Guha, in India After Gandhi, argues that while leaders changed, the mindset of governance remained colonial: rule over the people rather than rule for the people. The Emergency of 1975–77 exposed this reality. Even after the fall of Indira

Gandhi, when the Janata Party came to power, people hoped for real change. Instead, old patterns re-emerged—corruption, centralization, and authoritarianism. The colonial skeleton remained; only the flesh had changed.

Noam Chomsky's analysis of modern democracies applies here: real power lies not with the voters but with an "elite consensus." In colonial India, this consensus was formed in London; today, it is formed in New Delhi among politicians, corporate tycoons, and bureaucrats. The people merely legitimize their rule every few years by voting.

Colonial exploitation was clear: raw materials were taken cheaply from India, processed in Britain, and sold back at high prices. India was drained of wealth systematically. But has this changed?

Today, instead of British traders, it is Indian corporates who hold the wealth. The nexus between state and capital remains as strong as ever. Thomas Piketty, in Capital in the 21st Century, notes that capital and power always reinforce each other. In India, tax systems and policies favour the wealthy, while the middle class carries the heaviest burden. The poor are kept dependent on subsidies, while the rich find loopholes to evade taxes.

In colonial India, elites lived in lavish clubs and bungalows while ordinary people toiled under heavy taxation. Today, the elite reside in gated communities and luxury enclaves while the majority struggles with EMI, rent, and rising costs. The names have changed, but the hierarchy has not.

Arundhati Roy, in Field Notes on Democracy, observes that India's democracy retains the colonial mindset: resources belong not to the people but to power. Whether it is land, forests, or minerals, policies are crafted to benefit a select few. The British looted for the empire; today's elite loot for themselves.

During colonial rule, dissent was crushed. Speaking against the government could get one branded a seditionist. Newspapers were censored, gatherings were banned, and surveillance was constant. What is different today?

The language has changed, not the reality. If you speak against the government, you are called “anti-national.” Sedition laws, once used by the British, remain in use today. Peaceful gatherings face prohibitory orders, lathicharge, and arrests. During colonial times, it was bullets at Jallianwala Bagh; today, it is Section 144, FIRs, and digital surveillance.

Ramachandra Guha reminds us that in a democracy, dissent is essential. But in India, dissent is often treated as treachery. Arundhati Roy notes that the state has perfected the art of silencing opposition through legal and procedural means rather than open violence. In colonial times, the bullet was the weapon; today, it is the bureaucratic notice.

Even the media landscape reflects this continuity. The colonial state censored newspapers; today, tweets and posts are deleted. The colonial state employed spies; today, digital surveillance tracks every citizen. The machinery of control has become more sophisticated but no less oppressive.

Shashi Tharoor, in An Era of Darkness, writes that the British Raj's most enduring legacy was not just railways or buildings but a system of power that kept some Indians above and many Indians below. That hierarchy persists today.

Independence was not the breaking of chains but the passing of keys. The same colonial lock remains. Ministers, bureaucrats, and MLAs occupy the seats once held by governors, collectors, and zamindars. The middle and lower classes remain at the bottom, crushed under taxation, bureaucracy, and fear.

Mahatma Gandhi had warned that true freedom was not merely freedom from foreign rule but freedom from fear and injustice. If independence is merely the raising of a flag, then yes—India is free. But if independence means equality, justice, and the courage to live without fear, then India has never truly been free.

The problem is not just that colonial structures were inherited; it is that they were never dismantled. The police, the courts, the tax system, the bureaucracy—all remain colonial in spirit and function. They serve the powerful, not the people.

Real freedom will not come from changing rulers or celebrating anniversaries. It will come from changing structures, dismantling hierarchies, and reclaiming institutions for the people. Until then, independence will remain a myth, and the people of India will remain prisoners in a cage whose paint has changed but whose bars remain as strong as ever.

True liberation cannot come from nationalism or the nation-state. It cannot emerge from any system built on domination—whether colonialism, communal nationalism, monarchy, dictatorship, or even democracy in its present form. For in every such order, power is structured to rule over people, not to serve them. As long as we live within these cages, power will remain the master and humanity the subject. Until we dare to imagine and build a world beyond rulers and ruled, 15 August will remain not a celebration of freedom, but a reminder of chains merely repainted.

Nationalism has sometimes played a constructive role in history, but today it is one of the greatest obstacles to human progress. It is an outdated story that must be left behind. Until we break the chains of false national identity, wars and injustice will not end.

Law

The aphorism "Justice is blind" sits at the core of modern legal consciousness. In courtrooms, textbooks, and popular imagination, the image of Lady Justice—with her eyes covered, scales in one hand and a sword in the other—reinforces the belief that the law is impartial, treating everyone equally, without regard to identity, status, or bias. Through this metaphor, law is presented as a neutral and objective system, one that operates solely on facts and rules rather than power, wealth, recognition, or emotion. This image has become so deeply internalized that we often place the law beyond questioning. Yet, at this very point, a basic but uncomfortable question arises: if justice is truly blind, why is injustice so consistently predictable?

Empirical reality shows that legal outcomes are far from random. Who gets arrested, who remains in jail during trial, who can afford bail, and who secures competent legal representation—all these factors are strongly correlated with social position. Poor, marginalized, and powerless individuals disproportionately come into contact with the criminal justice system, while the powerful have mechanisms within the system for protection, delay, and escape. If the law were genuinely context-free and impartial, such patterns would not persist. Understanding this contradiction requires viewing law not as a moral abstraction, but as a philosophical and institutional construct.

Jurisprudence begins here—by interrogating the authority of law rather than taking it as natural or self-evident. Law is not a natural force that exists on its own; it is a human-made system developed within historical, political, and economic conditions. The statement "Justice is blind" is not a descriptive fact but a normative claim—an ideal that law projects about itself. Its primary function is not to guarantee justice, but to normalize obedience. When law is perceived as neutral and rational, obeying it seems logical and morally safe, and challenging it appears irrational or destabilizing.

The blindfold metaphor becomes misleading. Blindness is treated as a symbol of neutrality, whereas in reality it signifies the elimination of context. When law ignores context, it does not deliver justice; it merely executes procedure. Declaring a rich and a poor individual "equal before the law" may reflect formal equality, but not substantive equality. When bail depends on wealth, trials become a form of punishment, and legal expertise is a market commodity, the law's blindness becomes institutional indifference rather than fairness.

This claim of neutrality also serves a strategic function: diffusion of moral responsibility. The legal system legitimizes its coercive power—police, imprisonment, surveillance—through "due process." Once violence is legal, it ceases to appear as violence; it is framed as order and necessity. Judges follow rules, police enforce orders, and prisons execute law—within this chain, no actor perceives themselves as a moral agent. Responsibility dissolves into the system.

Human societies have never accepted obedience without justification. In every era, authority has required some moral or metaphysical foundation so that its commands are internalized not merely as coercion, but as "duty." In pre-modern societies, this foundation was largely religious. Law was understood as divine command—either directly from God or through God's representative. The distinction between sin and crime was blurred.

Violating a rule was not merely an act against the state, but against the cosmic order. In this framework, obedience was rooted more in faith than fear: people obeyed because they believed God was watching, not simply the law.

As modernity challenged religious authority, a vacuum emerged. Scientific rationality, Enlightenment thought, and secular politics gradually eroded the legitimacy of divine law. Yet authority itself did not disappear; it transformed. Where God once sat, the state now sits. Where priest and scripture once held sway, legislature and constitution have replaced them. "God says so" became "Law says so." The object of obedience became secular, but its structure—command, duty, punishment—remained intact.

The most interesting aspect of this transformation is that law inherited not only authority from religion, but its moral aura as well. Law projects itself not merely as a collection of rules, but as the guardian of order, stability, and social good. Just as religion elevates its commands as sacred and beyond question, law presents its commands as necessary and inevitable, immune to critique. In this process, law becomes more than a technical system; it becomes a moral institution—without explicitly using moral language.

The judge's role functionally mirrors that of the priest. Both act as interpreters of authority. Just as the priest interprets divine will, the judge interprets the constitution and statutes. Both have discretion, and both justify decisions through appeal to a higher legitimacy. Thus, the ritualistic nature of courtrooms is no accident—robes, formal language, elevated benches—all symbolize authority, creating distance and reverence. Law maintains its power not only through coercion, but through ceremony and symbolism.

With this shift, the distinction between sin and crime is only superficial. Sin, within a religious framework, was against the soul; crime, within a secular framework, is against the state. In both cases, the individual act is framed against an abstract authority. Moral complexity is compressed into legal categories; intention, circumstance, and social context become secondary, while rule violation becomes primary. In this way, law depoliticizes moral responsibility rather than personalizing it. Structural injustice becomes an individual crime, and obedience is rewarded as a virtue.

It is also noteworthy that secular law, while presenting itself as separate from religious dogma, performs a remarkably similar psychological function. Religion produced compliance through fear of divine punishment; law achieves the same through fear of legal punishment. Religion emphasized eternal consequences; law emphasizes immediate ones. The goal is identical: predictable behavior, controlled populations, and stability for authority. The difference lies only in law presenting itself as rational and scientific, making it socially more acceptable.

Law is commonly understood as a fixed and self-evident system, as if it has always existed and will remain unchanged. School textbooks, civics lessons, and legal institutions present law as a set of rules that must be followed simply because they are "law." In this framing, the origin of law, its purpose, and its beneficiaries fade into the background. For a lawyer, law is an operational tool: statutes, precedents, and procedures. For a philosopher, law raises deeper questions: what authority grants such power to demand compliance, and why do we regard it as legitimate?

Jurisprudence does not view law merely as a collection of rules; it sees law as an institutionalized form of command. Law is the system through which certain actors—legislatures, courts, and state apparatus—define binding norms for the population and impose sanctioned consequences for violating them. In this definition, morality becomes secondary, and enforcement becomes primary. Law is effective not because it is always just, but because it is backed by coercive power. Police, prisons, and surveillance are not accidental by-products; they are structural pillars.

At this point, it is essential to distinguish between law and justice. Justice is an ethical aspiration—fluid, contextual, and contestable. Law is a formal mechanism—rigid, codified, and enforceable. While they often overlap, they are not inherently identical. History repeatedly demonstrates that law can operate against justice and still remain legally valid. Slavery, segregation, colonial rule, and caste-based exclusions were not merely social practices; they were maintained through fully legal systems. Assuming that what is legal is automatically just is a dangerous conflation, one that transforms obedience into a moral virtue.

Another crucial aspect of law is its abstraction. Translating human conflicts into legal language flattens their political and moral dimensions. Structural exploitation becomes individual disputes; systemic violence is reframed as "law and order" issues. In this process, power relations are naturalized. What should have been political debate becomes legal technicality. In this way, law depoliticizes disagreement and reframes resistance as illegality. Obedience here is not mere compliance; it becomes morally desirable under the guise of civic responsibility.

Law's claim to legitimacy operates largely through procedure. If a rule is made through "proper process"—even if participation in that process is unequal—the rule is considered valid. This is how law's authority becomes self-reinforcing. Law justifies its legitimacy through law itself: parliament has power because the constitution says so, and the constitution has authority because the law says so. This circularity makes challenging authority psychologically and practically difficult. Authority functions as a closed system, deriving legitimacy not from external ethics but from internal consistency.

This structural framing creates the illusion of neutrality. Because law formally applies to all, it appears fair. Yet the gap between equality of application and equality of impact remains hidden. The same law applied to vastly unequal social conditions reinforces inequality rather than correcting it. Law may not create inequality, but it stabilizes it. This stability is celebrated as "order," though it merely freezes existing power relations.

In response to natural law's moral ambiguity, legal positivism emerged—a framework that deliberately separates law from morality. The central claim of legal positivism is deceptively simple and powerful: law is what is enacted by a proper authority through the proper procedure. Whether a law is just or unjust is secondary; its source and procedural validity are primary. If a rule comes from a sovereign authority and follows established legal processes, it is law, regardless of moral content. The appeal of this approach lies in its clarity and predictability, avoiding the chaos of moral disagreement. Yet within this strength lies legal positivism's most dangerous weakness.

Legal positivism frees obedience from ethical reflection. When law is disconnected from morality, compliance becomes a technical duty rather than a moral choice, for both citizens and institutions. "I am just following the law" becomes a powerful self-exculpatory statement. History shows that some of the most severe injustices were implemented through precisely this logic—not because people were cruel, but because they were compliant. When law is deemed legitimate solely through procedure, opposing authority appears not only illegal, but irrational.

The subtle effect of legal positivism is to blur the gap between legality and legitimacy. What is legal automatically seems acceptable because the system has validated it. In this framework, injustice becomes a policy problem rather than a moral one, something to be corrected through future amendments. Present suffering is deferred in the name of procedural patience. Phrases like "stay within the system," "follow the process," and "let the courts decide" cease to be promises of justice; they become instructions for obedience.

This approach has deep institutional effects. Judges are imagined as mechanical appliers of law, neutrally implementing statutes and precedents. This fiction renders judicial discretion and bias invisible. When a judge produces an unjust outcome, blame shifts to the system: "the law is such." Legal positivism dissolves moral responsibility, transferring it from individual actors to an abstract system. Law becomes an autonomous machine, in which no one sees themselves as accountable.

As a corrective to the mechanical clarity of legal positivism, legal realism emerged as a disruptive intervention. Legal realists confront an uncomfortable truth: law is not what is written in statute books; law is what judges actually do in cases. For them, law is not an abstract system but a lived practice—one that operates through human actors, and therefore cannot be free from their biases, experiences, and social positions. Legal realism directly challenges the myth that "justice is blind," insisting that law operates with eyes—and those eyes are human.

The central insight of legal realism is that judicial decision-making is not a purely logical or deductive exercise. Judges do not merely apply rules; they interpret, choose, and sometimes creatively expand or restrict them. In this process, a judge's class background, political ideology, moral worldview, and lived experience silently influence outcomes. Two judges reading the same law may reach different conclusions—and often do. If law were genuinely neutral and self-executing, outcomes would not vary so consistently. Legal realism exposes this variability and thereby destabilizes the claim of law's neutrality.

From this perspective, the gap between "law in books" and "law in action" is not accidental, but structural. Statutes and precedents provide a framework, but real power lies with those who apply them. The courtroom is not an abstract moral space; it is a social space where language, demeanor, respectability, and credibility matter. Who speaks, in what accent, and with what confidence subtly influence legal outcomes. Legal realism demonstrates that law is not merely a system of rule-following, but also a system of perception management.

Another disturbing implication is that judicial discretion is unavoidable. No matter how detailed the law, it cannot exhaustively cover every situation. Gaps always remain, and it is judges who fill them. Discretion implies power—and power is always unevenly distributed. When discretion is hidden beneath the myth of neutrality, accountability becomes difficult. A judge's decision becomes "law," and the law's decision becomes an "objective necessity."

Rights are commonly regarded as the most potent symbol of modern freedom. Constitutions, declarations, and legal charters present rights as if they are innate to humans—inalienable, inherent, and universal. Terms such as "human rights," "fundamental rights," and "natural rights" reinforce the impression that rights preexist the state, and that the state's role is merely to protect them. Yet when rights are examined through the lens of legal reality, an uncomfortable contradiction emerges: if rights are truly birthrights, why does their effective existence depend on state recognition?

Within legal systems, rights only become meaningful when they are enforceable, and the power of enforcement rests exclusively with the state. This implies that the practical status of rights is determined by the very institutions that rights are theoretically meant to limit. When the state "grants" a right, it simultaneously positions itself as the gatekeeper of that right. Rights, therefore, cease to be absolute; they become conditional—dependent on citizenship, legality, behavior, and often obedience. A law-abiding citizen experiences their rights fully; a dissenter experiences them as negotiable or restricted.

Here, the distinction between rights and permissions begins to blur. While permissions are always contingent upon authority's discretion, rights are theoretically beyond it. Yet when rights operate through law, they increasingly behave like permissions. The right to protest is valid only so long as it does not create inconvenience; freedom of speech is tolerated only so long as it does not directly challenge power; the right to movement exists only until the state declares an emergency. In this way, the scope of rights silently shrinks without formal revocation.

It is also noteworthy that the discourse of rights often manages inequality rather than redresses it. While formal rights may be granted equally to all, the capacity to exercise them is unequal. For a powerful individual, a right functions as a shield; for a marginalized person, the same right becomes a paper promise. Courts and legal procedures are theoretically open to all, but in practice, access is contingent upon time, money, and literacy. The universal language of rights, rather than challenging existing hierarchies, often stabilizes them.

From the perspective of legal positivism and legal realism, the meaning of rights becomes even more fragile. Their interpretation depends on judicial discretion, and their enforcement depends on the executive's will. A right considered fundamental today may be suspended tomorrow in the name of an amendment, exception, or emergency. History repeatedly demonstrates that, in moments of crisis, rights are the first to retreat while authority expands. This pattern makes it evident that rights do not operate in opposition to power, but within its framework.

Thus, viewing rights as unconditional freedom is a comforting illusion. Rights exist, but they are fragile. They function not against the state, but through the state.

Following this, law itself is often presented as a moral domain, as if obedience is a virtue in itself. Civics textbooks, political speeches, and legal discourse assume that citizens comply with the law because they perceive it as legitimate, just, or socially necessary. Yet deeper analysis from jurisprudence and social psychology reveals that consent is rarely the primary driver of obedience; conditioning is. Individuals do not internalize law because they agree with it, but because from childhood, they are taught to perceive law as natural, unavoidable, and morally superior. Fear—of punishment, social exclusion, or state-sanctioned violence—is the most obvious mechanism.

Fines, imprisonment, police action, and legal harassment transform law from a neutral rulebook into a coercive structure. Modern legal systems, however, rely not solely on fear. If obedience were purely fear-based, resistance would be more visible. Therefore, law merges itself with morality, so that obedience feels internally chosen rather than externally enforced.

Social conditioning plays a key role. Schools teach children to become "good citizens," instilling punctuality, discipline, rule-following, and respect for authority as ethical virtues. Questioning authority is framed not as curiosity, but as indiscipline. Exams and grading systems reward compliance and penalize deviation. The end result of this training is that challenging the law feels immoral and antisocial, even when the law itself is unjust.

Social contract theory offers a philosophical justification, framing obedience as rational consent. Individuals voluntarily surrender certain freedoms in exchange for collective security. Yet this “voluntary” aspect is largely fictional. No individual signs this contract in the real world, nor does a meaningful opt-out exist. Law applies automatically from birth, and consent is assumed rather than chosen. Social contract thus functions as philosophical justification rather than a reflection of lived reality.

Utilitarian justifications further normalize law obedience in the name of efficiency. Compliance is framed as necessary for the “greater good,” even when individuals suffer injustice. This logic, however, ignores asymmetries of power: the definition of the “greater good” is often set by ruling institutions, while individual dissent is framed as inconvenience or threat.

Psychologically, obedience becomes habitual. Studies such as Milgram’s experiments demonstrate that individuals comply with authority even when it contradicts personal ethics. Uniforms, courtrooms, and formal language create an aura of authority, shifting responsibility from the individual to the system. “I was just following the rules” becomes a common moral escape.

Hence, when asked why people obey the law, the answer cannot be reduced to fear, consent, or morality alone. Obedience is a deeply engineered behavior: it begins with fear, is normalized through education, and is justified ideologically. The process is so subtle that obedience comes to feel like freedom.

Punishment is often perceived as the natural extension of justice—as if the violation of law inherently warrants suffering. Legal systems justify punishment in moral terms: as a response to crime, a closure for victims, or protection for society. Yet closer analysis through jurisprudence and critical legal theory reveals that punishment is not a neutral instrument for delivering justice; it is a disciplined mechanism of social control that reinforces obedience and suppresses dissent.

Classical retributive theory conceives punishment as a moral repayment by the wrongdoer for their actions. The "eye for an eye" logic presents justice as balance. However, this theory rests on a problematic assumption: that the infliction of suffering can restore moral equilibrium. Modern ethical frameworks question whether intentional pain can ever constitute justice, or whether it is merely revenge cloaked in rational language.

Deterrence theory justifies punishment as a preventive measure: punishment is a warning, instilling fear of consequences to discourage future lawbreaking. Empirical evidence, however, shows that deterrence is influenced more by the certainty of punishment than by its severity. Harsh penalties disproportionately affect marginalized communities, while powerful actors often evade or negotiate punishment. In this sense, punishment undermines the principle of equality.

Incapacitation theory isolates individuals to protect society—through prisons, detention centers, and surveillance. Yet this approach treats human beings as sources of problems rather than participants in social contexts. Crime is abstracted from its economic, social, and psychological determinants, reducing systemic issues to individual pathology. Prisons thus become warehouses of social exclusion rather than spaces for rehabilitation.

Rehabilitation theory frames punishment as a tool for reform, appearing humane on the surface. Yet it assumes the state decides which behaviors are "normal" and which are "deviant." Rehabilitation often becomes conformity training: individuals are adjusted to the system rather than challenging systemic injustice. Reform, in practice, becomes obedience rather than autonomy.

Michel Foucault and similar thinkers highlight that punishment is embedded within broader networks of discipline and surveillance. Modern punishment is not only physical but psychological, bureaucratic, and digital. Criminal records, background checks, social stigma, and perpetual suspicion extend punishment beyond sentencing. In this sense, punishment is not an event but a long-term identity that keeps individuals under control throughout their lives.

Thus, defining punishment solely as a response to crime is intellectually insufficient. Punishment functions as a political technology: it maintains inequality, disciplines dissent, and rewards obedience. So long as punishment is unquestioningly accepted in the name of justice, law functions more as a power structure than as an ethical system. True justice begins when punishment is viewed not as inevitable, but as a choice—prompting the questions: whose safety, whose order, and at whose cost?

Justice is commonly regarded as the ultimate purpose of law. Courts, punishments, rights, and procedures all presuppose that the legal system's goal is to deliver justice. Critical examination, however, shows that justice is neither fixed nor universally accessible. More accurately, justice emerges as a negotiated outcome between power relations, institutional limits, and social hierarchies rather than existing above them.

Traditional legal thought associates justice with neutrality and fairness. "Equal treatment before the law" is a foundational promise. Yet equality is procedural rather than substantive. Laws may apply equally, but people do not approach the law from the same social position. Class, caste, gender, education, and access to resources fundamentally shape the experience of justice. The promise of justice is abstract; its delivery is profoundly unequal.

Distributive justice links fairness to the distribution of resources and opportunities. Legal systems, however, often protect rather than challenge distributions. Property laws, inheritance rules, and corporate protections stabilize existing inequalities. When inequality is normalized through legal frameworks, justice shifts from redistribution to maintenance of order. Justice becomes protection for the powerful and compliance for the vulnerable.

Procedural justice claims that fair processes yield just outcomes. Yet processes are not neutral. Language barriers, legal complexity, delays, costs, and institutional biases make access selective. Courtroom decorum and technicality render common citizens passive spectators while trained professionals control the narrative. Here, justice becomes submission rather than participation.

Corrective justice seeks to repair harm through victim compensation and offender accountability. Yet criminal justice systems rarely heal victims. Victims become objects of litigation, with their suffering mediated through the state. Offenders solve systemic problems through punishment, while social harm remains unaddressed. Justice here becomes transactional rather than relational.

Critical legal studies view justice as ideology—a moral narrative legitimizing the law's power. Justice language absorbs resistance: even protest is acceptable only in procedural formats. Radical demands are translated into moderate procedural claims, turning justice into a safety valve that protects the system from meaningful challenge.

Therefore, viewing justice as an ideal or illusion is insufficient. Justice is dynamic, contested, and negotiated—it can serve both liberation and domination. Law does not define justice; it decides which injustices are tolerable. True justice begins when we stop equating law with justice and recognize justice as an ongoing ethical struggle, where conscience matters more than obedience.

Power in law does not exist merely as coercion; it exists in definition. Law determines which acts are "legal" or "illegal," which demands are "reasonable" or "extreme." These boundaries are not arbitrary; they align with dominant social interests. When property violations are criminalized but exploitation is legal, law protects power, not morality. Political choices are embedded in neutral legal terms.

Legal language abstracts concrete suffering. Terms like "due process," "public order," and "national interest" translate human consequences into technical necessities. Evictions, layoffs, detentions, and surveillance are justified as lawful actions, even though their impact is uneven and often irreversible. The law does not deny suffering; it normalizes it.

Institutions depersonalize power. Judges, police, and administrators appear as functionaries rather than as individually responsible actors. "I am only following the law" becomes an ethical shield, diffusing accountability and anonymizing harm. Power operates facelessly, making resistance difficult.

Law determines political outcomes without political debate. Electoral laws shape representation, labor laws limit bargaining, and security laws criminalize dissent—all in the name of procedure. By preempting debate over illegality, law confines politics within predefined frameworks.

Critical perspectives argue that law's most effective function is to naturalize power. Inequality is perceived not as a political failure, but as legal reality. "The law says so" becomes the final answer rather than the starting question. Law restricts imagination—only solutions deemed legal are thinkable.

Hence, law should not be understood merely as a rulebook. Law is a political architecture that organizes reality, constrains choices, and normalizes obedience.

Modern legal systems do not merely regulate actions; they also construct identities. The idea of the "good citizen" is subtly defined through law—a person who is rule-following, compliant, and non-disruptive. Here, citizenship becomes not just a legal status but a moral certificate. Those who obey the law are considered "good"; those who question it become suspect. In this process, morality gradually reduces to legality.

The moral compass of a good citizen is not internal but external—defined through statutes, notifications, and permissions. Legal compliance replaces ethical judgment. People stop asking what is right and focus only on what is allowed. Moral responsibility shifts from the individual to the system. If something is legal, it is assumed ethical, no matter how socially damaging its impact may be.

Education, media, and bureaucracy together reinforce the prototype of the good citizen. Textbooks glorify law-abiding behavior as a civic virtue, while civil disobedience is presented as an exception or historical anomaly. Protests are considered respectable only if they occur with permission, follow designated routes, and do not create disruption. Resistance is domesticated through regulation.

The most problematic aspect of this myth is that legality is substituted for morality. Slavery, colonial exploitation, caste-based discrimination, and gender oppression were historically legal, yet the "good citizen" narrative normalized them. Those who followed the laws perceived themselves as ethical.

The good citizen myth delegitimizes dissent. People who stand against the law are labeled irrational, emotional, or anti-social. Their arguments are rejected on procedural grounds rather than substance. The logic of "right in the wrong way" renders resistance morally weak. In this way, demands for systemic change become trapped within the system's own rules.

Morality

Morality is generally considered the foundation of human society through which categories like "right" and "wrong," "good" and "bad," "pure" and "impure" are created. Almost every society claims that its moral system is universal, natural, and derived from human reason. Morality is often presented as an essential condition for human civilization—almost as if, without moral rules, society would descend into chaos, violence, and inhumanity. Yet, while this claim seems intuitive, it is highly questionable. If morality were truly universal and natural, why then do we see such vast differences in moral codes across time, place, and culture?

The biggest problem with morality lies in its definition. When we say "this is wrong" or "this is right," it is often unclear on what basis we make that claim. Is the basis nature? God? Reason? Society? Or power? In most cases, the basis is not clarified, because morality is presented as a self-evident truth beyond question.

If we look closely, morality is not a rule of nature but a rulebook created by human society. Nature does not make distinctions between "good" and "bad." Morality only arises where social life exists. It is not a natural truth, but a social construct.

History shows that morality has not been static. Actions considered moral in one era were declared immoral in another. Slavery was once deemed moral and natural; today it is considered an inhumane crime. Denying women education, caste discrimination, religious violence—these were all once presented as "moral duties." If morality were truly eternal and unchanging, such shifts would not be possible. The fact that morality changes demonstrates that it adapts with time and power structures.

Morality is often called "the voice of human reason," but this is misleading. Reason is individual, while morality becomes collective rules. When a society declares a behavior moral, it does not merely suggest—it expects compliance. Morality, in this sense, becomes a means of collective discipline, not independent reasoning. If an individual disagrees with it, they face guilt, shame, ostracism, or punishment.

Thus, morality does not only convey knowledge of right and wrong, but becomes a powerful tool for controlling behavior. Morality is often linked to culture. We are told, "This is against our culture" or "This is wrong according to our tradition." Yet culture itself is a historical process, not a fixed truth. Culture develops along with power, resources, and dominance. The morality of the influential class or group becomes "social morality." Morality, therefore, is never neutral; it reflects power structures.

It is also important to note that morality is often selective. The same society that condemns theft as immoral glorifies looting during war as heroism. The same culture that condemns killing as sin may call killing for the nation a noble sacrifice. This shows that morality changes according to interests and identity, not truth. This flexibility makes morality more political than ethical.

Another feature of morality is that it abstracts the individual from their context. When an action is declared moral or immoral, circumstances, compulsion, social pressure, and historical reasons are often ignored. The individual is blamed alone, while the structures within which they act remain invisible. In this way, morality becomes a tool for concealing structural injustice.

It is not necessary to say that morality is entirely meaningless. The problem is not its existence, but its sanctification. When morality is declared the ultimate truth, it is placed beyond questioning. And whatever is beyond questioning can become a tool of oppression. Morality becomes dangerous when it presents itself in the name of humanity, yet in reality protects power.

Humans lived for millions of years in small tribes and groups. In early human societies, survival was not possible through individual strength, but through group cooperation. A lone human was weak in the wild—neither the fastest, strongest, nor most dangerous. But by living in a group, following rules, and trusting one another, survival became possible. This is where the basic ideas of morality developed. Behaviors that supported the survival of the group were deemed "good." Behaviors that threatened the group were declared "bad."

In this sense, morality was not a truth-based system, but a utility-based system. Evolution did not care whether something was morally right or wrong; it only mattered whether the behavior increased or decreased survival chances. Hence traits like honesty, loyalty, obedience, and sacrifice became moral virtues because they made the group stable and predictable. Conversely, betrayal, selfishness, dissent, and rule-breaking were deemed immoral because they threatened group cohesion.

Evolutionary psychology shows that certain moral instincts are hardwired in our brains—like the sense of fairness, anger at cheaters, and desire to punish norm-breakers. These instincts are not the product of conscious philosophy, but of natural selection. Tribes that did not punish rule-breakers became internally unstable and lost to more organized groups.

In this context, the role of punishment is also crucial. Punishment's main purpose was not justice, but deterrence. It sent the message that breaking rules had costs. Hence morality became linked with fear—shame, guilt, and social exclusion. These emotional tools regulated behavior without formal law.

Here we see the deep connection between morality and obedience. Obedience was not accidental; it was an evolutionary requirement. The more obedient survived in the group; the rebellious were isolated or eliminated. Over time, obedience became a virtue, and disobedience became immorality. Another point is clear: morality has always been ingroup-based. Moral rules were strict for "our own," and relaxed or reversed for outsiders.

Murder was wrong—but only within the group. Killing or looting outsiders was not considered wrong; sometimes it was heroic. This double standard was not hypocrisy, but an evolutionary logic. Morality was never universal; it always came with boundaries—tribe, clan, caste, religion, nation.

As societies grew complex, morality became institutionalized. Initially it was informal, enforced through customs and traditions. Later, religion codified it, and the state formalized it as law. But its evolutionary core remained the same: "behavior control for system stability."

The evolution of moral language is also important. Words like "good" and "evil" were not neutral descriptors, but emotional labels designed to bypass logic and trigger immediate reactions. When a behavior is called "evil," rational discussion becomes difficult. This is an evolutionary shortcut: act quickly, don't overthink.

Hence morality often works against reason. When the group feels threatened, moral panic arises. Logic is slow; morality is fast.

Evolution made morality fast because speed mattered for survival, not accuracy.

In modern society, the same morality becomes dangerous. A system once designed for survival is now used for power. States, religions, and ideologies press our evolutionary moral buttons to extract obedience. Guilt, shame, pride, honor—these moral emotions are biologically deep-rooted.

This does not mean humans are cruel; it means morality is not neutral by design. It easily aligns with power because its evolutionary function was to regulate behavior.

If morality were truly universal, it would not change with time, culture, or power. Yet we see that as economic and political structures change, morality updates. What was immoral yesterday may be acceptable today; what is moral today may be shameful tomorrow. This flexibility does not indicate strength, but the constructed nature of morality.

Thus, from an evolutionary perspective, studying morality is both dangerous and liberating. Dangerous because it shatters sacred myths; liberating because it grants the right to question morality. If morality is a human survival strategy, we can redesign it—to reduce harm, not to enforce obedience.

Blindly following morality may feel natural, but it is not morally justified. What evolution created, defending in its name is wrong. Evolution also produced rape, violence, and dominance—but we do not call them moral. Likewise, morality should not be sacred, but accountable.

The Earth we inhabit is a microscopic part of this vast universe. Our planet is a tiny speck of dust orbiting an average star—the Sun. And the Sun itself is not special; there are billions of such stars in our galaxy. Our galaxy is not unique; billions of galaxies exist in the observable universe. Compared to this unimaginable vastness, human existence is almost invisible.

The universe has existed for billions of years. Stars form and explode, galaxies collide—all without intention or moral concern. Humans appeared only a few thousand years ago. If the universe were a 24-hour clock, human civilization would appear in the last few seconds. Believing the universe was created for us, with morality written at its center, is not scientific; it is a psychological projection. It is childish arrogance, created to avoid accepting our fragility.

We are not special observers outside nature. We are part of it. Like trees, animals, and insects, humans are biological organisms. Our bodies are made of the same chemical elements produced in stars: carbon, oxygen, iron, calcium. We are literally stardust, not magical creations beyond natural laws. We are the result of evolution—a long, slow, blind process aimed at survival, not morality.

Evolution has no moral compass. It does not ask who is good or bad; it only "observes" who survives and reproduces. If cooperation aids survival, cooperation evolves; if aggression helps, aggression evolves. Both are equally valid for nature. Assuming morality is part of nature's design is a fundamental misunderstanding. It is crucial to understand: nature does not care—about our happiness, suffering, or morality.

Good and bad do not exist in nature. They are human concepts. We use these labels to organize reality, regulate behavior, and stabilize society. But when we elevate these labels to cosmic truths, problems begin.

IDENTITY AND PRIDE

The use of terms such as 'identity' and 'pride' has become so common in modern society that their meanings are often assumed to be self-evident. It is therefore necessary to first clarify what is meant by identity. In common understanding, identity refers to the answer we give to the question, "Who am I?" However, this answer is more often collective than individual—such as religion, caste, nation, language, gender, or culture. This indicates that identity is less self-chosen and more socially assigned.

Academic sociology and anthropology demonstrate that identity is not a natural or biological entity, but a social construct. At birth, a human being is merely a biological organism; transforming that individual into a "Hindu," "Muslim," "Brahmin," "Indian," or "Bengali" is the work of society and its institutions. Identity refers to the process through which society fits individuals into predefined categories.

At this point, an important distinction must be understood:

1. "Individual identity": formed through personal experiences, choices, and consciousness.
2. "Collective identity": assigned on the basis of birth, lineage, geography, or tradition.

This chapter primarily focuses on collective identity, because it is far more useful to power structures.

Identity is often presented as "natural"—for example, religion or nation is portrayed as timeless and eternal. However, historical and scientific evidence shows that these identities are relatively recent developments. Nation-states are only a few centuries old. Organized religions emerged within specific historical contexts.

Caste systems were systematically rigidified during particular historical periods.

Therefore, calling identity “natural” is an ideological claim, not a scientific one. Labeling something as natural places it beyond questioning. Identity, however, does not possess such a nature. The clearest characteristics of constructed identity are that it is assigned at birth, exiting it comes with social penalties, and questioning it is treated as offensive. Together, these three features turn identity into a powerful mechanism of control.

It is now necessary to examine pride. Pride is generally viewed as a positive emotion—associated with self-confidence, dignity, or self-respect. Academic analysis, however, does not treat pride as a single emotion. Instead, it distinguishes between two fundamentally different forms of pride, each with distinct psychological and political consequences.

The first form is "self-respect" (healthy confidence). This develops through an individual’s own actions, efforts, and ethical choices. It is earned, reflective, and tied to personal responsibility. It does not require comparison with others, nor does it depend on diminishing someone else.

The second form is "group pride" (collective ego). This is attached to inherited identity—such as birth, lineage, community, nation, or culture—without any personal achievement. This pride is not effort-based but birth-based. The critique in this chapter is directed at group pride, not self-respect.

The core logic of group pride is: “I am special because I belong to a particular group.” Within this logic, individual merit becomes irrelevant. The source of pride shifts from personal action to collective identity. As a result, pride is acquired without effort and defended without responsibility.

The function of pride is not limited to providing happiness or confidence. It plays a deeper psychological role—ego protection. When an individual's personal life is insecure—due to economic instability, social marginalization, or lack of personal achievement—group pride functions as emotional compensation. It provides temporary psychological stability without addressing real problems.

This pattern explains why history repeatedly shows that regions with greater material insecurity often exhibit more aggressive forms of identity-based pride. Pride allows individuals to feel that even if their personal situation is weak, their identity is "great." Personal failure is covered by collective greatness.

When pride becomes permanently attached to identity, identity ceases to be merely a label. It becomes the emotional core of the individual. At this stage, questioning identity is no longer a logical or intellectual exercise but an emotional threat. Critique is experienced as an attack.

The direct consequence is that criticism is perceived as insult, disagreement as hostility, and reform as betrayal. This process gradually blocks rational thinking. Individuals begin defending their identity even when it is objectively harmful, irrational, or oppressive.

The most important point of the conceptual foundation is that identity and pride are not politically neutral. Both function as raw materials for power. Identity divides people into fixed categories, and pride attaches emotional loyalty to those categories.

This combination provides power structures with three major advantages. First, people divide themselves voluntarily. Second, instead of questioning authority and systems, people invest their energy in defending their identities. Third, people become entangled in symbolic and emotional conflicts rather than focusing on real material issues such as education, healthcare, and inequality.

According to evolutionary evidence, the majority of 'Homo sapiens' history was spent in small hunter-gatherer groups. These groups typically consisted of around 30 to 150 individuals—what anthropologist Robin Dunbar conceptualized as 'Dunbar’s Number'. At this scale, social life was entirely direct and personal. Everyone knew one another personally, social roles were flexible, cooperation was essential for survival, and hierarchies were temporary and situational.

In this context, “identity” was not a symbolic or abstract concept. There was no religion, no nation, no caste. To define a person meant answering practical questions: Who is useful? Who is trustworthy? Who cooperates? Identity was grounded in performance and behavior, not birth or abstract labels.

This leads to a fundamental conclusion: the human brain did not evolve for identity, but for cooperation and survival. Evolutionary psychology recognizes that humans possess an in-group/out-group differentiation tendency. However, the original function of this tendency was limited—to detect immediate threats, manage resource competition, and make rapid trust decisions.

This instinct evolved for small, face-to-face groups. When the same instinct is applied to modern societies—comprising millions or even billions of people—problems emerge. Modern identities are abstract and symbolic, demanding loyalty toward people one has never personally encountered. This represents an 'evolutionary mismatch': an ancient brain mechanism being applied to a social scale for which it was never designed.

A major turning point in evolutionary history was the advent of agriculture. Food surplus enabled permanent settlements, rapid population growth, stabilized hierarchies, and the concentration of resource control in the hands of a few. At this stage, the old system of direct personal trust collapsed. Power now required new tools to manage large populations. It is here that symbolic identity systems—such as caste, religion, lineage, and later nationality—emerged.

Pride is an emotion that was originally adaptive. In evolutionary terms, pride functioned to reinforce achievement, signal social status, and reward cooperative behavior. However, this pride was tied to individual achievement—successful hunting, skill development, group protection, or meaningful contribution. Modern identity-based pride reverses this logic.

This form of pride is not evolutionarily meaningful; it is psychologically addictive. The brain receives the dopamine associated with achievement without effort. This is precisely why identity pride spreads so easily—it offers reward without work.

Modern neuroscience shows that identity pride activates the brain's reward system. Group validation triggers dopamine release through likes, slogans, chants, and symbols. As a result, individuals become emotionally dependent on identity reinforcement. At the same time, when identity is perceived as threatened, the amygdala is activated, rational processing is suppressed, and a fight-or-flight response is triggered.

This is why criticism of identity ceases to be a logical debate and becomes an existential threat. For the brain, it is experienced as a matter of survival, regardless of whether any real danger exists.

From an evolutionary perspective, the human brain prefers simplicity. Complex realities—such as economic systems, structural inequality, or historical nuance—are cognitively costly. Identity offers simple, emotionally satisfying explanations: "We are good," "They are bad," and "Someone else is responsible for our suffering." This simplicity fits comfortably within the brain's evolutionary constraints. Consequently, identity-based explanations gain popularity even when they are factually incorrect.

An important point must be recognized here: what was once evolutionarily adaptive has become destructive in modern society. The costs of identity pride are not merely psychological; they manifest as large-scale violence, genocide, religious wars, nationalist conflicts, and systemic discrimination.

These are essentially scaled-up versions of small tribal conflicts, where the damage increases exponentially. The brain remains the same, but power and weapons have changed.

Human beings are fundamentally social organisms. Psychological research shows that belonging is a basic psychological need—on par with food and safety. When individuals feel that they belong to a group, they experience emotional security. Identity directly addresses this basic need.

However, there is a crucial distinction. Belonging means being accepted, whereas identity means being classified. Modern societies do not provide belonging; they provide classification. Identity creates the 'illusion' of belonging without real human connection. This illusion is precisely what makes identity so psychologically effective.

Social Identity Theory (Henri Tajfel) explains how individuals construct self-image through group membership. For many people, the answer to "Who am I?" is derived from "Who are we?"

This process involves three core steps. First is 'categorization', in which people divide themselves and others into social categories. Second is 'identification', where individuals form emotional attachment to their category. Third is 'comparison', in which one's own category is portrayed as superior to others.

This is where pride emerges. Pride arises from comparison, and comparison is impossible without hierarchy. As a result, identity-based pride almost always implies some form of superiority.

The primary psychological function of pride is ego protection. When an individual's personal life involves economic instability, low social respect, or lack of personal achievement, the ego becomes vulnerable. To manage this vulnerability, the mind turns to group pride. Group pride allows the individual to feel: "I may be personally weak, but my identity is strong."

This compensation is temporary, yet emotionally powerful. That is why identity pride remains psychologically strong despite being logically weak.

Psychological studies indicate that individuals who aggressively defend their identity are often internally insecure. Secure individuals do not need to constantly assert or loudly proclaim their identity. For insecure individuals, identity functions as an emotional shield.

This explains a recurring pattern: greater insecurity leads to greater identity aggression; lower self-worth leads to stronger group pride. Identity-based aggression is not a sign of strength but an indicator of internal fragility. When identity pride fuses with the ego, the psychological response to criticism fundamentally changes. Questioning identity is no longer a rational disagreement; it becomes an existential threat. Psychology refers to this process as 'identity-protective cognition', in which protecting identity takes precedence over evaluating truth.

Identity pride also creates a binary worldview. This mode of thinking functions as a cognitive shortcut. Rather than engaging with complex social realities, the mind prefers simple moral categories. As a result, identity narratives tend to be simplified rather than nuanced.

This binary thinking reduces empathy as well. When "they" become abstract and dehumanized, the emotional weight of their suffering diminishes. Through this psychological mechanism, ordinary individuals are able to justify extraordinary cruelty.

Another significant psychological effect of identity pride is 'moral outsourcing'. Individuals transfer moral responsibility to the group: "What we are doing must be right, because we are on the right side." In this mindset, individuals no longer feel personally accountable for their actions.

This psychology is ideal for power structures, because it detaches individuals from moral responsibility for their decisions and behavior.

When strong evidence challenges identity, cognitive dissonance emerges—an uncomfortable mental state. To reduce this discomfort, individuals may reject the evidence, discredit its source, or adopt conspiracy theories.

Abandoning identity is psychologically painful because it requires accepting that one was wrong, risking social belonging, and confronting a loss of meaning.

The human brain is not designed for truth; it is designed for survival. Its primary goals are threat detection, ensuring safety, and maintaining social belonging.

From an evolutionary perspective, rational thinking—associated with the prefrontal cortex—is a relatively recent development. In contrast, emotional and threat-processing systems such as the amygdala and the limbic system are evolutionarily older, faster, and more dominant. When identity is activated, these older neural systems take control, and rational processing becomes secondary.

Neuroscientific studies consistently show that when an individual's core identity is challenged, the amygdala is activated, stress hormones such as cortisol are released, and the fight-or-flight response is triggered. In this state, the brain is not operating in a mode conducive to logical discussion. For the brain, criticism of identity is no longer a question of "Who are you?" but a signal of "Will you survive?" This is why identity-based debates become emotionally explosive.

The prefrontal cortex is responsible for reasoning, critical thinking, and impulse control. However, when emotional arousal is high—as during perceived identity threat—prefrontal cortex activity is suppressed. In such conditions, even logically strong arguments are difficult to process objectively, because the emotional brain has already interpreted the situation as dangerous.

Identity pride also activates the brain's reward system. When individuals encounter group symbols, hear slogans aligned with their beliefs, or experience group approval, dopamine is released—producing pleasure and motivation. This dopamine provides an effort-free reward. Individuals feel as though they have achieved something without any real achievement. This mechanism explains why identity pride becomes psychologically addictive.

A well-established concept in cognitive science is "confirmation bias"—the brain's tendency to accept only information that supports pre-existing beliefs. In the case of identity, this bias becomes significantly stronger because the belief is not merely an idea but an extension of the self. As a result, the brain either ignores conflicting information, discredits its source, or interprets it as hostile intent. The outcome is that the same evidence leads different identity groups to entirely opposite conclusions.

Research also shows that higher education does not necessarily make individuals more rational in matters of identity; in some cases, it makes them more biased. This phenomenon is known as "identity-protective cognition". Here, intelligence is not used to seek truth but to defend identity, construct stronger justifications, and build complex rationalizations. This is why education alone cannot resolve identity fanaticism.

The human brain becomes fatigued by complexity. Topics such as economic systems, historical injustice, and structural inequality are cognitively demanding and require sustained analytical effort. Identity narratives, by contrast, are simple and emotionally satisfying. Because the brain naturally prefers simplicity, identity-based explanations feel more appealing—even when they are factually incorrect.

Neuroscience also demonstrates that humans are wired for emotional contagion. Group chanting, crowd slogans, and collective outrage activate mirror-neuron systems. At this stage, the individual brain gradually dissolves into a group brain. Facts target rational circuits, whereas identity resides in emotional circuits. When the two come into conflict, emotional circuits usually prevail. At this point, truth becomes secondary, and loyalty becomes central.

The majority of human history unfolded during the pre-agricultural phase. In hunter-gatherer societies, populations were small, social relations were face-to-face, authority was temporary and situational, and resources were largely shared collectively. At this stage, no rigid or institutionalized identity systems existed. Individuals established their value through behavior, skills, and cooperation. There were no permanent "upper" or "lower" categories. Historical evidence therefore suggests that identity rigidity is directly proportional to population size—as groups grew larger, identities became increasingly fixed and hierarchical.

With the advent of agriculture, this balance collapsed. Food surplus led to permanent settlements, and populations began to grow rapidly. As numbers increased, the face-to-face trust system broke down. This is where identity acquired its practical function. Rulers could no longer know individuals personally, yet governance was still required. Classification became necessary—who would work, who would rule, who would pay taxes. At this moment, the core function of identity emerged: "classification as control".

The caste system of the Indian subcontinent is a textbook example. Caste provided power with three major advantages. First, labor was permanently assigned—occupation became fixed by birth. Second, inequality appeared natural and normal. Third, resistance was framed as a violation of religious duty. Here, identity functioned less as a cultural phenomenon and more as an economic and political mechanism. Caste transformed exploitation into tradition, making the system self-sustaining.

The rise of religion is also deeply connected to this historical context. Early belief systems were fluid and local, but as states and empires formed, religion became institutionalized. Priestly classes defined morality, sanctified obedience, and granted divine legitimacy to rulers. Religion provided identity with moral armor. Identity was no longer merely a social category; it became sacred truth. At this stage, dissent was no longer just a political crime—it became blasphemy.

The nation is a relatively recent invention. Medieval societies identified with their village, ruler, or faith—not with a nation. With the emergence of the nation-state, language was converted into identity, borders were declared sacred, and history was transformed into selective narratives. To make national identity emotionally powerful, flags, anthems, martyrs, and textbooks were systematically introduced. Identity thus became a powerful tool for imagined unity.

In the industrial era, mass production gave rise to mass identity. To control workers, mobilize armies, and efficiently collect taxes, shared identity became a necessity. This was the period during which nationalism exploded, racial theories gained popularity, and identity pride began to be used as a political weapon. Identity was no longer a side-effect of governance; it became a core strategy.

The twentieth century provides the most violent evidence of identity's destructive potential. Nazism was based on racial identity, Fascism on extreme national pride, and genocides on ethnic and religious identities. These were modern identities, not ancient ones. Technology, bureaucracy, and mass propaganda weaponized identity on an industrial scale, allowing abstract ideas to unleash unprecedented levels of violence upon real human beings.

Early human belief systems were fluid. People simultaneously followed multiple deities, local spirits, and rituals. Belief was personal, contextual, and flexible. However, as societies became larger, more settled, and more hierarchical, belief was institutionalized. With this transition, the role of religion fundamentally changed—from belief to identity. At this stage, religion ceased to be a form of spiritual inquiry and became a mechanism of social classification.

Religion sacralizes identity. To be sacred means to be beyond question. This is religion's most powerful psychological weapon. By making identity sacred, religion renders it immune to rational critique. As a result, questioning religious identity is not treated as disagreement but as blasphemy.

Religious identity is often accompanied by narratives of being "chosen" or "special." These narratives become an exceptionally powerful source of pride. Individuals come to feel that they stand on the side of a cosmic truth. This pride is unrelated to personal achievement; it emerges purely from belonging. Through this process, an illusion of moral superiority is created, in which "we" are naturally righteous and "they" are inherently misguided or evil.

One of religion's most distinctive features is that it transforms obedience into a moral virtue. Secular power enforces obedience through coercion and punishment, whereas religion enforces obedience through reward. The psychological effect of this framing is that individuals voluntarily surrender their autonomy. Obedience is driven not by fear of punishment alone, but by the desire for afterlife rewards, divine approval, and social acceptance.

Religion reinforces identity not only through pride, but also through fear and guilt. Concepts such as hell, sin, karma, and divine punishment function as psychological regulators. Their primary role is to regulate behavior without the need for constant physical surveillance. At this stage, the need for external control diminishes, and religion becomes a self-regulating identity system.

Historically, religion has legitimized social hierarchies—such as caste systems, gender roles, slavery, and monarchy. Hierarchy receives divine sanction. Once inequality is made sacred, resistance is no longer merely a political act; it is reframed as immoral and sinful.

Rituals function as the psychological engine of religion. Practices such as collective prayer, chanting, fasting, and festivals generate shared emotional experiences. Both neuroscience and psychology show that collective rituals strengthen emotional bonding to an irrational degree. Identity pride becomes automatically attached to this bonding, without the need for conscious reasoning.

Religion presents itself as a source of peace, yet history is saturated with religious violence. This contradiction becomes intelligible when religion is viewed not as belief, but as identity. Beliefs can coexist; identities compete. Once religion becomes identity, conflict becomes almost inevitable.

In modern societies, as traditional religious authority weakens, religion asserts itself more aggressively as identity. Political actors use religion as a tool for mobilization, vote-bank consolidation, and emotional distraction. In this context, religion ceases to function as a medium of spirituality and becomes a device for mass psychological management.

Despite scientific progress, religious identity survives because science does not provide existential comfort. Science asks questions and accepts uncertainty, whereas religion offers ready-made answers—even if they are false. This emotional certainty is precisely why religious identity continues to maintain its grip in a rational, modern world.

Political theorist Benedict Anderson described the nation as an “imagined community.” Here, 'imagined' does not mean false or fictitious; it means that the nation is never directly or personally experienced by any individual. The nation is felt through symbolic narratives—maps, flags, anthems, textbooks, and shared stories. Most citizens never meet one another, yet they experience an emotional bond. This is why people are even willing to die for the nation. This paradox can only be understood through the framework of identity psychology.

National identity is not ancient. In medieval societies, people identified with their village, their ruler, or their religion—not with a nation. The rise of the nation-state occurred primarily in the eighteenth and nineteenth centuries, when industrialization produced mass populations, centralized states required large-scale loyalty, and armies, taxation, and uniform laws needed legitimacy. In this context, nationalism emerged as an emotional adhesive, enabling millions to emotionally attach themselves to an abstract, impersonal state.

The core emotion of nationalism is pride—national pride. This pride is not based on individual achievement but on birthplace, historical myths, and selective collective memory. Individuals come to feel: "I belong to this nation, therefore I matter." This pride becomes particularly effective during periods of personal insecurity—such as economic stress, unemployment, or social inequality.

The most dangerous feature of nationalism is that it converts political obedience into moral duty. Questioning state decisions is labeled "anti-national," "traitorous," or "unpatriotic." In this way, democratic disagreement is transformed into emotional blackmail, where loyalty replaces logic.

Nationalism glorifies sacrifice. Soldiers, martyrs, and bloodshed are framed through sacred narratives. The intrinsic value of individual life is gradually subordinated to the abstract honor of the nation. Historically, wars are driven largely by economic and political interests, yet they are justified in the name of national pride. Nationalism prevents a fundamental question from being asked: "For whose power are people actually dying?"

National identity becomes fully meaningful only when an "outsider" exists. This is why nationalism frames immigrants as threats, treats minorities with suspicion, and portrays internal dissenters as enemies. Boundary policing is an essential feature of nationalism. The sharper the distinction between "us" and "them," the more intense the pride becomes.1

In a highly diverse society such as India, nationalism becomes even more complex. Amid economic inequality, unemployment, and social fragmentation, nationalism revives civilizational pride, converts historical myths into political tools, and often fuses with religious identity. This fusion makes dissent increasingly risky, because criticism is framed not merely as political disagreement but as cultural offense.

National pride frequently diverts attention away from real issues. Emotional symbols—such as the flag, the anthem, and glorified history—overshadow material concerns. The noise of pride silences the demand for accountability, allowing power structures to operate without challenge.

"Birth-based identity" refers to an identity that is determined not by an individual's actions, effort, or conscious choices, but purely by the accident of birth. Categories such as caste, race, ethnicity, and lineage fall within this framework. This form of identity pride is the most irrational, because neither pride nor shame is earned here—neither through achievement nor through ethical choice.

The basic assumption behind this type of identity is: "'I am valuable because I was born here, or because I was born into this group.'"

This assumption contains two fundamental logical flaws. First, birth is a biological randomness—no one has any control over it. Second, assigning moral or social value to randomness is non-rational. Yet societies have historically turned birth into the foundation of hierarchy.

The origins of caste and race systems were not spiritual or cultural, but political. Whenever resources became limited, power concentrated in a few hands, and labor needed to be systematically exploited, elites created birth-based categories. Whether it was the caste system or racial segregation, the objective was the same: to create a ruling class and make the rest accept obedience as their destiny. Declaring birth as destiny became one of the most efficient tools of power.

The Indian caste system is often justified in the name of spirituality and tradition, but in reality it functioned as a rigid labor-division system. It blocked social mobility and gave religious sanction to exploitation. What work a person would do, what they could study, whom they could marry—all of this was decided at birth. Individual potential and ability became irrelevant.

Race is a myth constructed in the name of science. Modern genetics has clearly established that biological human races do not exist. Genetic variation is greater within so-called races than between them. Yet race-based pride justified slavery, moralized colonialism, and even rationalized genocide. Whether white supremacy or the Aryan myth, the logic remains the same: birth equals superiority.

The psychological attraction of birth-based pride is that it requires no effort, carries no risk of failure, and provides instant ego satisfaction. If someone is proud of their caste, race, or lineage, they no longer need to achieve, grow, or engage in self-reflection. This pride gradually becomes a substitute for individual growth.

Where some inherit pride, others inherit shame. They internalize low self-worth and begin to see their limitations as "natural." This system does not merely create oppression; it normalizes oppression inside the minds of its victims.

Science's position on this is absolutely clear: intelligence is not linked to inherited caste or race; talent is broadly evenly distributed across the human population; differences arise only from opportunity, which is unevenly distributed. Birth-based identity turns this opportunity gap into a biological explanation. By presenting inequality as natural, the entire system is made to appear innocent.

Today, openly defending caste or race is no longer socially acceptable, yet these systems continue to survive—through surnames, marriage preferences, housing discrimination, and neutral-sounding terms like "cultural fit." Pride is no longer loud, but more subtle, and therefore more durable.

The primary function of language is communication. However, in modern societies, language is no longer merely a medium of communication; it gradually becomes a marker of belonging. Language defines "us" and "them," signals social status, and draws group boundaries. When someone says, '"This is our language,"' they are not merely describing a way of speaking; they are declaring ownership and exclusion.

Language pride becomes problematic when one language is declared superior, others are labeled "impure," "backward," or "less refined," and loyalty is demanded on the basis of language. History shows that linguistic pride often fuses with nationalism, enforces cultural uniformity, and renders minorities silent or invisible.

In a multilingual society like India, the role of language pride becomes even more sensitive. Here, language is projected as proof of civilization, a symbol of national unity, and a marker of cultural purity. In this process, speakers of non-dominant languages gradually begin to feel "less national," and linguistic diversity is viewed not as a natural reality but as a problem. In such a context, language pride goes beyond cultural affirmation and becomes a political mechanism that measures belonging and loyalty.

In present-day India, language is frequently projected as proof of civilization, a symbol of national unity, and a marker of cultural purity, even though constitutionally no "national language" exists. Despite this, Hindi is given a default position in public institutions such as railways, banking, central government communication, and national-level examinations. Through this process, non-Hindi speakers receive an implicit signal that their linguistic identity is less aligned with the central imagination of the nation, and when they resist, they are labeled divisive or anti-national.

The discourse around the three-language formula reinforces the same logic. Officially, it is presented as a model of linguistic balance and choice, but in practice, non-Hindi states face greater pressure to learn Hindi, while there is no reciprocal expectation for Hindi-speaking regions to learn southern or northeastern languages. Through this asymmetry, linguistic diversity is treated not as a natural human reality but as an administrative inconvenience, where unity comes to mean linguistic conformity rather than voluntary coexistence.

Media and political narratives also operate with an implicit hierarchy, where the Hindi belt is portrayed as "real India," while other linguistic cultures are labeled regional, local, or peripheral. Languages such as Bengali, Tamil, Malayalam, Manipuri, or tribal languages like Bodo, Santhali, and Lepcha are framed not as civilization-building traditions but as cultural sub-identities. The psychological effect of this framing is that speakers of non-dominant languages gradually begin to see their own languages as low-status and having limited futures, undermining linguistic self-confidence.

Alongside this, another contradiction emerges: in public discourse, English is labeled colonial and anti-Indian, while actual power structures—such as the higher judiciary, corporate sector, policy drafting, and higher education—remain largely English-dominated. In this way, language pride becomes not an egalitarian movement but a tool of selective morality, where English is acceptable for elites and Hindi is imposed as a cultural duty on the masses.

Renaming drives and excessive Sanskritisation also become part of this ideological project, where Urdu, Persian, tribal, and mixed linguistic histories are erased to construct a homogenized cultural past. This process is not an organic evolution of language but a political attempt to purify history and identity through language. In the Northeast and tribal regions, this is even more visible, where despite constitutional recognition of languages, their effective use in administration, higher education, and employment remains almost negligible.

The cumulative effect of all this is that language no longer remains a neutral tool of communication, but becomes a silent citizenship test. Questions like "“You don’t know Hindi?”" cast doubt on a person’s national belonging, especially for migrants, students, and linguistic minorities. In a multilingual India, when language is politicized in the name of pride, diversity becomes a problem rather than a strength, and unity becomes an imposed performance rather than a lived reality. In this context, language functions not as a bridge but as a border—an invisible border, yet one that is deeply experienced on a daily social and psychological level.

Culture was originally a dynamic process—an evolving pattern of how people live, eat, think, and interact. But when culture is tied to identity pride, it becomes frozen. Tradition is made sacred, and change is seen as betrayal. This cultural conservatism stabilizes power structures, because change always poses a risk to authority.

Symbols are shortcuts of identity. Flags, scripts, traditional dress, and rituals compress complex histories and power relations into simple emotional triggers. Psychologically, the moment a symbol is seen, an emotional response is activated, critical thinking is bypassed, and the individual synchronizes with the group. This is why symbols are favorite tools of authoritarian and hierarchical systems.

The human brain often mistakes familiarity for truth. What is taught from childhood, repeated continuously, and presented with emotional charge begins to feel "natural." Language and culture use this familiarity to make identity unquestionable, without revealing that these are historical and political constructions.

Language not only creates identity, but also class. Accent, pronunciation, and vocabulary become false signals of intelligence and competence. Linguistic discrimination occurs in the name of education, where certain ways of speaking are considered "smart" and others "inferior." This linguistic elitism is not scientific; it is merely the result of social conditioning.

Cultural pride often stands against individual choice. Statements like "'In our culture this is not allowed,'" or "'Our tradition does not accept this,'" turn culture from a living framework into a control mechanism. Individual experience, consent, and autonomy become irrelevant, and conformity is turned into a virtue.

Science treats change as normal and necessary, whereas cultural pride sees change as a threat. This is why scientific reforms are labeled as cultural attacks, and rational critique is dismissed as "Western influence" or a "foreign agenda." Cultural pride protects stagnation, not growth.

Propaganda

Every major institution—be it a religion, a political party, or a corporation—relies on propaganda to spread its ideas. Yet the most powerful and the most dangerous form of propaganda is that disseminated by the state. Why? Because no other entity possesses the tools and authority that governments do.

The first and most potent instrument is education. In most nations, the state controls the education system and uses it not primarily to nurture critical minds but to mold obedient citizens. From an early age, children are taught a version of history that glorifies their nation and vilifies others. They are trained to believe that dying for one's country is the highest virtue. They are not encouraged to question but rather conditioned to accept predetermined answers.

Across history and political systems, education has repeatedly functioned less as a means of cultivating critical consciousness and more as a mechanism for producing compliant citizens. In Nazi Germany, school curricula were explicitly redesigned to promote racial hierarchy, glorify the state, and normalize obedience to authority, while dissenting thought was framed as moral corruption. Imperial Japan similarly infused education with emperor worship and militaristic ethics, teaching children that self-sacrifice for the nation was the highest human virtue. During the Cold War, even liberal democracies such as the United States presented heavily curated narratives in which national actions were framed as inherently benevolent, slavery and imperial violence were softened or sidelined, and ideological alternatives were portrayed as existential threats rather than subjects for rational examination. The Soviet Union followed a comparable pattern from a different ideological angle, treating official doctrine as unquestionable truth and repeatedly rewriting history to align with party interests. In many post-colonial nation-states, including across South Asia and Africa, textbooks construct a singular national story that glorifies ancient heritage, suppresses internal diversity, and portrays war and sacrifice as heroic destiny rather than political failure. Authoritarian regimes like North Korea and contemporary China further demonstrate this logic by tightly controlling what may be taught, erasing inconvenient historical facts, and elevating leaders to near-mythical status. Across these diverse contexts, the pattern remains consistent: early emotional conditioning, selective history, glorification of national sacrifice, and the discouragement of fundamental questioning, revealing an education system designed not for intellectual liberation but for psychological alignment with state power.

The second weapon is the media—television, radio, newspapers, and increasingly, the internet. Governments control media either directly, through state-owned outlets, or indirectly, by exerting economic pressures such as advertising revenue and regulatory threats. The media decides what is visible and what is invisible, what is magnified into crisis and what is erased into silence. A lie repeated often enough begins to resemble truth; fear can be manufactured; hatred against particular communities can be cultivated; and leaders can be portrayed as saviors.

The third weapon is economic coercion, and it operates quietly but powerfully. Most people depend on their jobs, businesses, or professional networks for survival, and this dependence can be exploited to enforce conformity. In many contexts, speaking out against authority—or even expressing an unpopular opinion—carries the real risk of losing one's livelihood. For example, journalists in India have faced threats, loss of accreditation, or blacklisting for criticizing government policies or exposing corruption. Similarly, workers in China may face demotion, job termination, or even social repercussions for questioning the Communist Party, while in the United States, employees who protest company policies or unionize can encounter subtle retaliation or career stagnation. This fear produces a chilling effect: people conform outwardly, even when they disagree internally, because protecting their families and economic security outweighs the cost of honesty.

Economic coercion works hand in hand with psychological manipulation. Propaganda exploits the human need to belong, a core trait of social creatures. Our deepest fear is isolation, and this fear can be weaponized. Governments, institutions, and powerful groups frame the world as divided between "us" and "them"—our nation versus the foreigner, our religion versus the heretic, our race versus the outsider. In India, nationalist rhetoric during elections often portrays dissenters as unpatriotic or traitorous, making ordinary citizens hesitant to question popular narratives. Internationally, during the Cold War, Americans who questioned government policies risked being labeled "communist sympathizers," while in Nazi Germany, even minor acts of disagreement could lead to social ostracism or economic consequences. This social pressure ensures that even errors or lies endorsed by the dominant group are defended, because the cost of exclusion feels higher than the cost of truth.

Together, education, media, economic control, and human psychology form an invisible machinery of state propaganda. It creates the illusion of independent thought while guiding minds along pre-set pathways. People feel they are thinking freely, yet most of their opinions are shaped, limited, and filtered through systems designed to maintain power. The result is an intellectual cage, invisible but real, in which the boundaries themselves are presented as the full expanse of the world. This combination of economic fear, social pressure, and information control ensures that dissent remains rare and compliant conformity becomes the default, even in societies that pride themselves on liberty and free thought.

People often believe that whatever they think is their own. Every thought, every decision, every dream— as if it came entirely from their own will. But in reality, most people think what they have been taught to think. And the one who teaches them is not just a single person. It is an entire system. A system that is very old, very deep, and very cunning.

Controlling thought is more powerful than controlling with a sword. Because if you can make someone believe that whatever is happening is right, then you don't need walls to keep them in prison. You don't need handcuffs. You don't need a stick. They build their own prison. They follow its rules themselves, and then start believing that this prison is actually freedom.

When a child is born, the mind is like a blank page. And the process of writing on this page begins immediately. Family, school, television, religion, language, patriotism, society, neighbors, books, teachers, exams, advertisements—all slowly shape the mind into a format. This format is such that it suits the system. A format where no questions are raised, only answers are given. Where people are trained not to change things, but only to follow them.

It is said that we have freedom—freedom to think, to speak, to act. But think carefully. Does the mind really think what it wants to think? Most of the time, what we like has already been shown to us in some advertisement. The dreams we see are already planted somewhere. From career to marriage, from religion to nation—opinions are already formed, and it feels like we formed them ourselves.

This siege of thought is done so cleverly that a person believes they are free. But in truth, their freedom has become an illusion. The one taught patriotism never questions whether what they were taught is actually true. The one forced to memorize religious texts never asks why what is written is beyond questioning. The one told to become an engineer or doctor in the name of career never asks whether this is the only path in life.

In reality, raising questions is the very first form of freedom. But the system has twisted thinking so much that the one who asks questions is branded as a traitor. And the one who doesn't question is considered the ideal citizen, the true devotee, the good child, and the successful person.

So the question is: who controls this thinking? The answer is simple—the ones in power.

For example, if someone questions religion, they are called sinful, godless, atheist. If someone questions national policies, they are called anti-national. If someone talks about marriage, gender, body, or the very structure of life, they are branded as lost, uncultured, or immoral. Meaning—whoever steps outside the limits of thought is cut off by society. And this fear is what keeps thought trapped within boundaries.

And the biggest traders of thought are those who decide what people should see, hear, read, and remember. From history books to news channels, from films to social media trends—everything is decided. Some things must be shown. Some things must be hidden. And some things must be repeated so often that they start to feel true.

The powerful don't just run the news. They run thought. And controlling thought means holding a person's entire life in their pocket. When an entire generation starts to believe that money is success, they are ready to do anything to earn it. When a society starts to believe that fair skin is beauty, people chase it blindly. When people of a nation start to believe that dissent is treason, then there is no hope left for change.

This trade in thought doesn't stay limited to the mind. It sells the soul too. Slowly, a person doesn't even realize that their mind is no longer their own. They laugh, they fear, they feel happy, they get angry—but behind all of this, they are not in control. They just react. As if someone is pressing buttons, and they are dancing to those buttons.

The day one realizes that what is running in their mind is not truly their own—on that day, real thinking begins. Otherwise, the whole life is lived according to someone else's plan, while it feels like everything was done by one's own choice. In truth, a human is most enslaved when they believe they are free. And these chains of thought, which are invisible, are the most dangerous of all.

Have you ever wondered whether the clothes you wear, the phone you buy, the shoes, perfumes, cars, or hairstyles—are really for yourself, or just for show? Most of the time it feels like the decisions are our own. But the truth is, what we like has already been decided somewhere else. The very path of thought that leads to our choices is a path designed by others. And it all happens very cleverly—without making us feel it, without force.

Take a very simple example: someone wears a ₹3000 T-shirt. The fabric is the same as a ₹300 one. But the logo, the brand, and the social value have turned it into a piece of "respect." Now it is no longer just cloth. It has become a status. And this "respect," which people believe is earned, slowly starts getting bought instead—through brands, styles, and displays. In reality, this game is not about respect at all. It is about fear. Fear that people might judge us as less. Fear of becoming a joke. Fear that someone might say—his phone is old, his shoes are cheap, he's just ordinary.

For the very rich, these things are everyday matters. Buying a new phone is no different than having a cup of tea. For the very poor, it is clear that they cannot buy such things at all—the distance between wanting and getting is too vast, so they don't even enter the game of display. It is the middle class that gets trapped. They want everything. But for each thing, a price must be paid. And this price is not only money. It is also self-respect, sacrificing real needs, and most of all—forgetting one's own identity.

People think the things they buy bring happiness. But in reality, those things only create a new target. As soon as you buy a branded watch, another brand is placed before your eyes. As soon as you get a car, another model is shoved into your vision. Before you can take a breath of relief, a new dream is planted. And this doesn't stop with outer things. Even the body, skin color, way of speaking, style of walking—everything is questioned. And to escape these questions, people start molding themselves into what the world wants.

Ask those who go to the gym—do they really go to stay fit, or just to show others? If no one were watching, would they work as hard? The problem today is that hardly anything is done for oneself anymore. Everything is done for social value. And the ones who create all this—the brands, the ads, the marketing companies—they know very well how huge the market of fear and show-off is. Everyone is only thinking: what will others think? And this very thought becomes life's biggest prison.

Think of a person buying a phone on EMI. Paying installments for 24 months just so they don't feel embarrassed in front of others. But imagine—if there were no one watching, no one judging—would that phone really be necessary? This system survives on the dangerous idea that humans must be hollowed out from within so that they seek their identity in outside things. The more a person buys, the more they feel like they've "become something." But deep inside, only a new fear grows: what next?

Each time, something new must be bought. Something new must be shown. Otherwise, the fear of "what will people say?" creeps in. And it all happens so smoothly that no one suspects it's actually a trap. Respect is no longer earned—it is bought in the market. And the market knows that the hunger for respect is the sharpest of all hungers.

With social media, this trap has only grown stronger. Now every photo, every story, every post sparks a new comparison, and people start believing that show is everything. The real question is not whether this is right or wrong. The real question is—are these choices truly yours, or just a habit of seeing yourself through the eyes of others? Until that is understood, a person keeps running an invisible race. A race with no finish line, no victory—only the exhaustion of trying to prove oneself.

And so, the first truth of this game is simple: respect is now for sale. And those trying to buy it are, every single day, selling something else—their time, their money, and most of all, themselves.

Every human carries a dream within. Someone wants to become "big," someone just wants to be happy, someone wants love, someone wants respect. And it is these very dreams that have been captured and turned into an entire marketplace. A marketplace that sells everything humans don't actually need—but makes them believe that without it, they are nothing. In truth, it is not dreams that are being sold. It is fear. Fear of failure. Fear of being alone. Fear of being left behind. Fear of being seen as less than others.

First, this fear is planted in your mind. And then, the cure for that fear is sold back to you in the market. Think about it. From school to social media, you are told that if you don't come first, your life will be ruined. If you are not fair-skinned, nobody will like you. If you don't wear branded clothes, no one will respect you. If you don't drive an expensive car, people won't take you seriously. What happens then? All these messages line up and fill you with fear. And then the very same companies that created the fear promise to cure it. It's like they poison you first—and then sell you the antidote. That is the real business.

Take a simple example: fairness creams. First, you are bombarded with the idea that fair skin is beauty. Every ad, every movie, every matrimonial site repeats this. Then, when you become dissatisfied with your own self, the market says—we have the solution. And that solution is sold—in a ₹300 tube. Now, the real question: if society never said fair skin is necessary, would anyone ever touch that cream? This is how it works with every dream. A dream is planted in you without your consent. Once it sits inside you, you throw your time, effort, and money into chasing it.

The powerful know very well that to control humans, only two things are needed: fear and greed. Show the fear, then sell the dream of escaping it. And once a person is trapped in that dream, they don't even realize what has happened.

Go deeper: take the education system. Every parent wants their child to succeed. But who defined success? The same system that first created the fear of failure. Now, when every child studies under the shadow of fear, coaching centers, career guides, motivational seminars—everything starts selling "cures" for that fear.

The same goes for social media. Everyone looks happy, rich, beautiful, perfect. But the ordinary person, struggling in life, begins to feel something is wrong with them. When in reality, what they are seeing is an illusion—filters, editing, planning, lies. Still, they believe it, and start chasing the same illusion. Instagram sells a dream, and behind it runs a billion-dollar industry.

The market has captured human emotions at their core—love, respect, security, identity. Then it twists them until people believe: if you want these, you must buy something. Want respect? Buy an new latest iPhone. Want love? Use expensive perfume. Want identity? Wear branded clothes. But are these things really necessary? No. Yet fear and comparison have convinced you that without them, you are incomplete.

The most dangerous part of this entire system is that humans are never given the chance to pause and ask: is this truly my dream, or is it someone else's? Because if they stop even once to think that way, the entire market could collapse. That is why you are kept running all the time. As soon as one dream is fulfilled, another is handed to you. Buy a house for yourself. Buy insurance for your children. Buy mutual funds for old age. And in this way, a whole life is spent—not in living your dream, but in running after someone else's.

And at the very end, when a person sits exhausted, they realize: perhaps they never saw their own dream at all. They only lived others' dreams, one after the other. The truth is, the seller never wants humans to be satisfied. Because if one day people say, I don't need anything more, the entire market will shut down. That is why fear must always be kept alive. As long as fear exists, the shop of dreams will keep running. And this shop, though it looks colorful from outside, is hollow within.

Since childhood, every child is sent to school with the belief that they will receive an education there. But in reality, what happens is not education—it is a kind of formatting. The brain is set up like a computer so that the individual can become part of a system that is already predetermined. The goal is not to create someone who questions, but someone who obeys.

School is a place where freedom of thought is not given. Nothing is truly taught—things are memorized. How many times has it happened that a child asks a new question, and the teacher gets irritated, scolds them, silences them? Why? Because schools don't want questioners. They want people who can repeat a fixed syllabus without using their own mind.

Now think—who made this syllabus? Did ordinary people sit and decide what children should learn? No. It is decided by those in power, and their first requirement is that people should not be thinkers—just parts of the system.

Schools never teach a small thing that how the real world works. There's nothing about taxes, banking, or reality checks. Instead, they teach the Pythagoras theorem, but not how an EMI works. So that when the child grows up, they repeat the same mistakes their parents did—falling into debt, following the system, never questioning if what they are doing is truly necessary.

In a classroom, everyone is made the same. Same uniforms, same answers, same way of thinking. Those who are a little different are called weak, backbenchers. And if someone is too different, they are labeled problematic. In reality, all of this is formatting—treating a human not as a human, but like a machine.

Think of it as a conveyor belt where every child is placed in line, and at every level their mind is trimmed and shaped. The fearful one becomes the ideal student. The rebel becomes the rude one. The one who questions is called confused. And the one who silently accepts everything is called successful.

The deepest impact of this shows up when the child grows up and starts working. The same cycle continues—do what the boss says, follow the rules, and most importantly, never question the system. That's why most people end up as workers, not thinkers. And those few who dare to think either remain alone or the system cuts them off.

Now let's talk about the real trick of this formatting—the trick that separates a person from their true self. When a child is constantly told, "You must be a topper, you must become a doctor, you must score marks," their mind becomes a target machine. They never even get the chance to look within themselves and ask: what do I want to become? What do I think? Where does my interest lie?

This way, an entire generation is created—one that holds degrees but not independent thought. They can make résumés but cannot ask questions. And when this generation joins the workforce, it produces the same kind of next generation.

Now imagine—what if schools actually taught children to think for themselves? To question what they see? To not blindly trust what everyone says? What would happen then? The system would break. Humans would no longer be slaves. They wouldn't just live for jobs—they would truly live.

But this is exactly what those in control of the system do not want. That is why schools are designed only to teach reading and writing, but not thinking. Schools are factories where "human resources" are produced, not humans.

And the cleverest part of this formatting is that a person is never even allowed to realize that something wrong has been done to them. They believe everything is fine. “This is life. Everyone lives this way.” But the truth is, their thinking has been twisted over so many years that questioning itself starts to feel wrong.

Whatever they are doing—it is not really their own choice. They are only doing what they have been taught. And this “teaching” has been given the name of education, while in reality it is only formatting—shutting down thought, stealing freedom, and keeping humans enslaved.

And once a person no longer trusts their own thinking, then anyone can rule over them however they want.

The deepest needs of a human being are identity, belonging, and trust. And it is precisely these three things that are most exploited—through religion and patriotism. These are the two most powerful emotions that have been used in every age to control people. The most striking part is this: when these forces are used, people feel as if they are thinking for themselves, while in reality their thinking has already been scripted.

Devotion is no longer a personal practice—it has become a performance. Hymns blaring on loudspeakers, livestreamed rituals going viral on social media, flags on every street corner—all of this is part of a religious stage show. What matters here is not faith itself, but how much one can display their religiosity. Notice who makes the most noise in this show—who carries the biggest symbols, who shouts the loudest, who condemns others the most. And why? For the crowd, for applause, for likes, for votes. But think about it: does true faith need to be proven by shouting? Does it need publicity?

Now let’s turn to patriotism. Patriotism is supposed to be a feeling where one does something meaningful for their country. But what has it been reduced to today? Putting a flag on your profile picture. Shouting on every issue that someone is “anti-national.” Never asking questions—otherwise you’ll be called a traitor. Meaning: anyone who points out flaws in the system is branded an enemy of the nation. Speak against corruption—traitor. Question unemployment—traitor. Criticize the justice system—traitor. And who decides what patriotism is and isn’t? Those in power—the ones who want ordinary people to stay silent behind the mask of nationalism.

Whenever a major scandal is exposed, soon after some religious issue is raised. Whenever governments fail, suddenly a national honor issue is pushed. Because they know—when people are angry or caught in religious fervor, they forget about real issues like inflation, unemployment, healthcare, education. That’s when a mask is placed in front of you—a mask of religion and patriotism. Behind this mask hide those who fear your questions. And by wearing this mask yourself, you silence your own voice, believing you are doing the right thing.

The most painful part is that the middle class is exploited the most in this game. Because they are the most emotional. They are trapped between their children’s school fees, their jobs, their parents’ medicines.

Just watch every TV debate, every social media trend, every political speech. Aren’t they all guiding your thoughts? Aren’t your fears, your beliefs, your identity being shaped by someone else? The entire show runs for one purpose: to stop you from thinking. To make you believe what you’re told. To accept whatever is shown as truth. So that you keep repeating the same mistakes. Never blame the system—always blame some external enemy, some “heretic” or “traitor.”

Modern life is exhausting. Jobs, traffic, relationships, money pressure—everything weighs heavy. And when people finally get a little relief, they cling to it. The easiest relief is entertainment. A man spends the whole day being scolded by his boss, stuck in traffic, suffocated by routine. Yet he stays quiet—why? Because he knows that at night, his mobile, his TV, his web series, his cricket match, or his Instagram reels are waiting for him.

Entertainment is no longer a hobby; it has been turned into a necessity. And when something becomes a necessity, it means it already rules over you.

But what does this entertainment give you?

Movies where the hero never loses and the world changes in three hours. TV shows that either sell fear or fake love. Social media where everyone pretends life is perfect—except yours. Cricket and reality shows designed to shift focus away from real issues and toward clapping for a script. The question isn't whether entertainment is bad. The real question is: is it killing your ability to think?

After The Mirror

The structures examined throughout these chapters—law, education, work, state, economy, morality—do not exist at a distance from everyday life. They are embedded within daily decisions, habits, fears, and aspirations. Obedience is not an isolated act performed in moments of submission; it is an environment within which modern life unfolds. Precisely because of this proximity, it is often the hardest thing to perceive.

The aim of this work has not been to argue that human beings are entirely unfree, nor to claim that a condition of complete freedom is attainable. Such binaries—free versus unfree—oversimplify a reality that is far more complex. What has been demonstrated instead is that freedom, where it exists, operates within conditions that are largely inherited rather than chosen. These conditions shape the range of what appears possible, reasonable, and permissible long before conscious decision-making begins.

The most effective form of obedience is not imposed through direct command. It does not announce itself through visible authority or explicit threat. It emerges when regulation is internalized—when individuals learn to govern themselves according to norms they did not design. At this stage, obedience no longer requires enforcement. It is sustained through habit, expectation, and the quiet discipline of imagination itself. What is considered "realistic" replaces what might otherwise be conceivable.

At this point, obedience ceases to feel like obedience at all.

This book makes no promise of awakening, nor does it suggest that awareness produces liberation. Recognition is not rupture. To see the structures that shape one's life does not dissolve them. Most individuals will continue to live within the same systems, often by necessity, sometimes by adaptation, and occasionally through the illusion of choice. This contradiction is not a personal failure; it is a defining condition of modern existence.

For this reason, 'Obediently We' offers no exit strategy.

History repeatedly demonstrates that attempts to impose final solutions frequently generate new systems of domination. Even resistance, when transformed into doctrine, tends to reproduce hierarchy and demand obedience of its own. Certainty, regardless of intention, has often proven to be one of authority's most reliable instruments. This book therefore refuses to replace one framework with another.

Its task has been more limited—and more precise. It has sought to render visible what ordinarily presents itself as natural.

To reveal contingency where inevitability is assumed. To expose structure where common sense claims neutrality. What follows this exposure cannot be determined here.

For some readers, the arguments presented may remain at the level of intellectual engagement—objects of agreement, disagreement, or critique. For others, they may generate a persistent discomfort, an unease that resists easy resolution. For a few, this discomfort may initiate subtle shifts in language, expectation, or perception. None of these responses are prescribed, and none are privileged. The book does not measure success by transformation, but by clarification.

Life after this book will not be radically altered by its mere completion. Work will continue. Compliance will persist. Compromise will remain unavoidable. To expect otherwise would be to misunderstand the nature of structural power. Existence within a system and distance from it are not mutually exclusive positions. The more consequential distinction lies elsewhere: "whether the system is seen or remains invisible."

Seeing does not liberate. But it alters responsibility.

Once structures are recognized, neutrality becomes difficult to sustain. Actions—however constrained, contradictory, or limited—no longer occur in ignorance of context. The phrase “this is simply how things are” loses its innocence. Obedience, once named, can no longer fully conceal itself as inevitability.

It is here that a different kind of responsibility emerges. Not one assigned by law, morality, or ideology, but one that arises from awareness itself. This responsibility does not dictate action, nor does it offer guidance. It merely refuses disappearance.

This book deliberately refrains from instructing the reader on what must follow.

Because once the structures are visible, the next step cannot be delegated. A mirror has been placed before the reader.

ELEVEN FIFTY
PUBLISHING